Unshakable: A 52-Week Devotional for Teen Girl Athletes

CHRISTIAN ENCOURAGEMENT AND BIBLICAL INSPIRATION TO OVERCOME ANXIETY, STAY FOCUSED, DEVELOP MENTAL TOUGHNESS, AND COMPETE WITH CONFIDENCE

GRACE WALSH

THE EMERALD SOCIETY

Contents

Unshakable   v

1. Compete from Identity, Not Approval   1
2. Purpose Over Popularity   7
3. Confidence That Doesn't Crumble   13
4. Worth Beyond Your Position   19
5. The Enough Mindset   25
6. Faith That Shows Up to Practice   30
7. Mind Renewal, Mindset Training   36
8. Courage to Be Seen Trying   42
9. Praise Without Pressure   48
10. Criticism Without Crumbling   53
11. The Next Play Mentality   59
12. Joy Is Strength   64
13. Compete With Clean Motives   70
14. Small Habits, Big Results   76
15. Effort Is Your Responsibility   81
16. Self-Control in the Moment   87
17. Doing Hard Things on Purpose   92
18. Consistency Over Mood   97
19. Focus: One Thing at a Time   102
20. Work Ethic Without Burnout   107
21. Steward Your Body   113
22. Preparation Beats Panic   119
23. Train Your Self-Talk   125
24. Integrity When No One's Watching   131
25. Being Coachable   136
26. Excellence With Peace   142
27. Calm Under Pressure   148
28. When Anxiety Shows Up   153
29. The Fear of Failure Trap   158
30. Playing Free   163
31. Confidence After a Bad Game   168
32. Bounce Back Faster   173
33. Control the Controllables   178

34. Strength With Kindness　　　　　　　　184
35. Team First, Ego Last　　　　　　　　　189
36. Handling Jealousy and Comparison　　　194
37. Lead Without Being Loud　　　　　　　199
38. When You Feel Unseen　　　　　　　　204
39. Letting Go of Approval　　　　　　　　209
40. Pressure to Be Perfect　　　　　　　　　214
41. Staying Humble When You're Winning　219
42. Forgiving Yourself　　　　　　　　　　224
43. Handling Conflict Like a Leader　　　　229
44. Setting Boundaries　　　　　　　　　　234
45. When You're Not Chosen　　　　　　　240
46. Identity Beyond Sport　　　　　　　　245
47. When You're Injured or Sidelined　　　250
48. Courage to Be Different　　　　　　　255
49. Finishing Strong　　　　　　　　　　　260
50. Trusting God with the Outcome　　　　265
51. Gratitude in Every Season　　　　　　　270
52. Your Next Season　　　　　　　　　　275

Keep Going, Girl　　　　　　　　　　　281

Unshakable

Lace up, girl, your season starts today,
Not just to win, but grow your own way.
Some weeks you'll shine, some weeks you'll shake,
But you'll learn how to rise from every break.

When pressure is loud and nerves feel real,
Breathe in faith, and don't backpedal.
You're stronger than doubt, bigger than fear,
God's with you, steady, always near.

So flip the page, bring your whole heart,
This is your journey, your fresh new start.
One week at a time, you'll find your way,
Unshakable, girl. Now go play.

♡

ONE
Compete from Identity, Not Approval

You don't have to earn your worth;

bring it with you.

But you are a chosen people... God's special possession.

— **1 PETER 2:9**

📖 You Are Not Your Stats

Sports can start to feel like a giant scoreboard for your whole life.

When you play well, you feel noticed and appreciated. When you mess up, it can feel like everyone suddenly has X-ray vision and can see your insecurity, your nerves, and that one mistake you will replay in your head at 2:00 a.m.

And it's not just the game. It's practice, tryouts, cuts, positions, coaches, teammates, parents, social media highlights, and even the quiet comparisons you make without meaning to.

Sometimes it can start to feel like this:

Good game = I'm worthy.
Bad game = I'm embarrassing.

But here's the truth God wants you to build your life on, especially as an athlete:

Your value was decided before you ever played a minute.

1 Peter 2:9 says **you are chosen**. Not "chosen if you score." Not "chosen if you start." Not "chosen if people clap."

Chosen. Period.

That means you don't have to perform for approval. You can perform from a secure identity. There's a huge difference.

. . .

When you play for approval, pressure owns you. You tighten up. You overthink. You chase perfection. You get crushed by criticism and addicted to compliments. When you play from identity, you're freer. You can take risks. You can bounce back faster. You can be intense without being terrified. You can care a lot without falling apart.

So this week, here's your goal:

Stop asking, "Am I good enough?"

Start reminding yourself, "I belong to God, and that doesn't change when I have a bad day."

🎯 Game-Day Mindset: The Approval Trap (and the Switch)

The Trap: "If I play well, I'll feel okay about myself."

The Switch: "I'm already secure, so I can play bold."

Quick self-check:

- Do you feel *extra* anxious when certain people are watching?
- Do you spiral after mistakes?
- Do compliments feel like oxygen?

If yes, you might be living on approval, and approval is the worst kind of fuel, because it runs out fast.

This week's cue phrase:

☑ **"Chosen, not chasing."**

Say it under your breath before practice, warm-ups, or tryouts.

Training Room Application: Practice the Identity Reset

Use this 60-second reset once a day this week (and anytime you feel the pressure spike).

1. **Breathe in (4 seconds), breathe out (6 seconds)**
2. Put a hand on your chest and say: **"God, my worth is secure in You."**
3. Repeat your cue phrase: **"Chosen, not chasing."**
4. Ask one simple question: **"What's my next right move?"** (Next rep. Next pass. Next lap. Next choice.)

That's it. No drama. No spiraling.

Just reset and go.

🌱 Mindset Reps Journal Time

🎯 Where do I feel the most pressure to "prove myself" (sport, school, friends, social media)? Why?

💭 What do I usually tell myself after I make a mistake? Would I say that to my best friend?

🍃 What does it look like for me to play free instead of playing afraid?

✏️ Write one truth statement I want to believe this season (example: *"My mistakes don't define me."*)

💬 If God could say one sentence to me before a game, what would it be?

_____
_____
_____
_____
_____
_____
_____
_____
_____
_____
_____

🙏 Prayer

God, You see me completely, on my best days and my worst days.

Help me stop chasing approval.

Remind me that I'm chosen and loved, even when I mess up.

Teach me to play with courage, joy, and confidence that comes from You.

When pressure rises, help me reset instead of spiral.

Amen.

Weekly Challenge: One Game, No Approval

Pick one practice or one game this week and try this:

- Before it starts, whisper: **"Chosen, not chasing."**
- During it, every time you make a mistake, say: **"Next play."**
- After it, write down 3 wins that aren't stats, like:

> "I encouraged someone."
> "I stayed calm after messing up."
> "I tried again instead of shrinking."

Prove to your brain that you can compete with heart without letting approval be the boss of you.

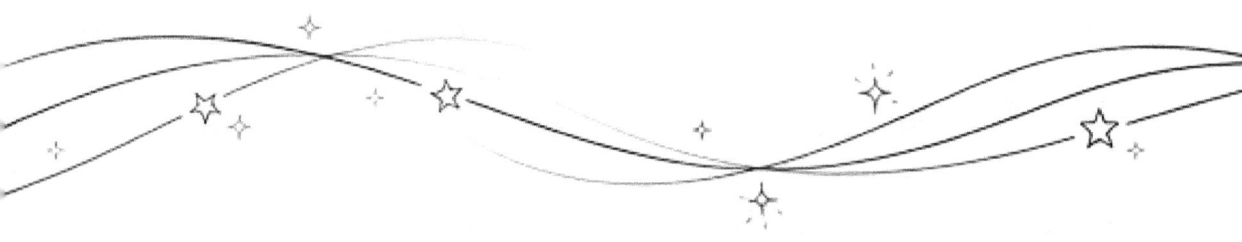

TWO
Purpose Over Popularity

You're not here to be liked by everyone;

you're here to live with intention.

Whatever you do, work at it with all your heart, as working for the Lord, not for human masters.

— **COLOSSIANS 3:23**

📖 When Being Liked Starts Driving

There's a weird pressure teen athletes don't always talk about out loud:

> Not just winning, but belonging.

Sometimes it feels like the real competition isn't even the game. It's the group chat. The team vibe. Who's in, who's out, who gets invited, who gets ignored. And if you're being honest, it can mess with your head more than a tough opponent.

You might catch yourself thinking:

- If I say the wrong thing, they'll think I'm annoying.
- If I don't laugh, they'll think I'm rude.
- If I try too hard, they'll say I'm "extra."
- If I don't try hard enough, I'm "lazy."
- If I do well, I'm "showing off."
- If I do badly… we don't even want to go there.

That's exhausting. And it turns sport into a popularity contest, where you're constantly adjusting yourself to fit into whatever gets the best reaction. But Colossians 3:23 offers a different anchor:

You're not living for everyone's approval. You're living with purpose.

Purpose means you have a "why" that doesn't change depending on who's watching. Popularity is unstable. One day people hype you up, the next day they're quiet. One teammate loves you, another decides you're "too much." Social media makes it worse because it teaches us to measure our worth by reactions such as likes, views, comments, streaks, replies.

Here's what God is offering you instead:

A steady reason to show up.

. . .

When your purpose is to honor God with your effort and your attitude, your life stops being a performance. You can still care about people (you're not turning into a robot), but you're not controlled by their opinions. Once you stop chasing popularity, you become lighter. You stop shrinking, you stop pretending, and you stop feeling like you need permission to be yourself.

This week, ask yourself:

Am I trying to impress, or trying to grow?
Am I trying to be chosen, or trying to be faithful?

You can't control who likes you, but you *can* control whether you show up with purpose.

🎯 Game-Day Mindset: Two Audiences

In sport, it can feel like you're always being watched by coaches, teammates, parents, crowds, even your own inner critic. But you get to choose which audience you're performing for:

Audience #1: People

- Changes constantly
- Rewards image
- Makes you anxious
- Leaves you empty

Audience #2: God

- Steady
- Values character + effort

- Brings peace
- Builds real confidence

THIS WEEK'S CUE PHRASE:

☑ **"I play with purpose."**

Say it before warm-up.

Say it when you feel yourself switching into "people-pleaser mode."

🏋 TRAINING ROOM APPLICATION: THE PURPOSE PLAN 3-MINUTE RESET

Do this once a day this week, before practice, before school, or before bed.

1. **Write your "why" in one sentence.** Examples:
    - "I want to honor God with my effort."
    - "I want to grow into a strong, steady person."
    - "I want to be the kind of teammate who lifts the room."
2. **Pick one purposeful action for the day:**
    - Encourage someone who's struggling
    - Hustle on the boring drills
    - Listen to your coach without rolling your eyes
    - Be kind without trying to be cool about it
    - Practice your skill even when no one notices
3. **Pray this simple line:** "God, help me live on purpose today."

Tiny habit. Big shift.

🪶 Mindset Reps Journal Time

💬 Where do I feel pressure to be "liked" the most? On my team, at school, online?

🔍 What changes about me when I'm trying to impress people? (No guilt, just awareness.)

⏱ Write your one-sentence "why" for this season. What do you want to become, not just achieve?

💭 When I feel left out or overlooked, what thought hits first? What truth could replace it?

○ What would change if I stopped trying to manage everyone's opinion of me?

_____
_____
_____
_____
_____
_____
_____
_____
_____
_____

🙏 Prayer

God, I don't want popularity to control me.

Help me live with purpose, even when it's uncomfortable.

Teach me to work with all my heart—not to impress people, but to honor You.

When I feel left out, ignored, or judged, remind me that Your love is steady.

Make me confident, kind, and focused on what matters.

Amen.

🔥 Weekly Challenge: The Purpose Choice

Pick one situation this week where you usually chase approval (team hangouts, group chat, practice energy, social media, etc.). Then do one purposeful thing instead:

- If you usually stay quiet to avoid judgment → speak kindness once.
- If you usually copy the vibe to fit in → be yourself without apologizing.
- If you usually scroll for validation → log off for one evening and reset your mind.
- If you usually perform for attention → work hard when no one's clapping.

Afterward, write one sentence:

> "What I chose today showed my purpose because…"

THREE
Confidence That Doesn't Crumble

Real confidence isn't pretending you're never nervous, it's knowing you're not alone in it.

My grace is sufficient for you, for my power is made perfect in weakness.

— 2 CORINTHIANS 12:9

📖 When You Don't Feel Like "That Girl"

Some days you'll walk into practice and feeling unstoppable. Other days, you might feel like your talent packed its bags and moved to another country without telling you. In sports, there's this unspoken rule that you're supposed to look confident at all times.

> Don't show nerves.
> Don't show doubt.
> Don't show emotion.
> Don't cry.

But confidence that depends on feeling strong *all the time* is fragile.

Because eventually you'll have a bad game. Or you'll make a mistake at the worst possible time. Or you'll get injured. Or your coach will be in a mood. Or your body will feel off. Or your mind will get loud.

And then what?

This is where God's version of confidence is different, and honestly, way more solid. In 2 Corinthians 12:9, God doesn't say, "Try harder so you never feel weak."

> He says, "My grace is sufficient for you."

And then He drops the plot twist: His power shows up best when we're weak. That means weakness isn't the end of your story; it's often the place God meets you most clearly.

So if you've been thinking, *"I shouldn't be struggling like this,"* here's your reminder: Struggle doesn't mean you're failing; it just means you're human.

Instead of seeing weakness as something to hide, you can see it as a moment to lean in and say:

"God, I need You right now."

That kind of confidence is quiet, steady, and real. Not the loud, showy kind that needs everyone to clap. It's the kind that can handle pressure, because it isn't built on pretending.

This week, you're not aiming to be fearless. You're aiming to be faith-filled, even when you feel shaky.

🎯 Game-Day Mindset: "I Have to Be Perfect" vs. "I Can Be Present"

Perfection mindset:

- Tight shoulders
- Overthinking
- Fear of mistakes
- Mood swings based on performance

Presence mindset:

- Breathe
- Lock in
- One play at a time
- Fast reset after mistakes

This Week's Cue Phrase:

✅ **"Grace makes me steady."**

When nerves hit, don't panic about being nervous. Just reset:

Breathe + cue phrase + next play.

🏋️ Training Room Application: The 10-Second Reset After Mistakes

Mistakes happen. The goal is to shorten the spiral time.

Try this reset immediately after a mess-up:

1. **Exhale hard once** (like you're blowing out a candle).
2. **Say in your head:** "Grace makes me steady."
3. **Pick one simple action:**
    - "Hands up."
    - "Sprint back."
    - "Eyes on the ball."
    - "Strong pass."
4. **Do the next right thing.**

You're teaching your brain:

mistakes don't get to steal the rest of the game.

📓 Mindset Reps Journal Time

😊 Where do I feel the most pressure to be "perfect" (sport, school, friendships)? Why?

🧠 What do I usually tell myself after I mess up? Write it down exactly.

✏️ Rewrite that self-talk with grace. What would I say to a teammate I care about?

💪 When have I shown strength *while* feeling nervous or unsure? (Proof you're stronger than your feelings.)

🙏 What is one area where I need God's help this week—and what would it look like to actually ask?

_____
_____
_____
_____
_____
_____
_____
_____
_____
_____
_____
_____

🙏 Prayer

God, You already know where I feel weak, insecure, or not enough.

Thank You that You don't shame me for it.

Your grace is enough for me—even on messy days.

Help me stop pretending I'm fine when I'm not.

Make me steady under pressure, quick to reset, and brave enough to keep going.

When I feel weak, remind me that You are strong in me.

Amen.

🔥 Weekly Challenge: Grace Over Spiral

This week, choose **one** moment where you would normally spiral (a mistake, a bad drill, a rude comment, a bench moment).

When it happens:

1. **Do the 10-second reset.**
2. **Say one truth out loud or in your head:** "God's grace is enough for me."
3. **After practice/game, write one sentence:** "What I learned about myself today was…"

Your goal isn't flawless performance. It's becoming the kind of athlete who can take a hit while keeping her heart steady.

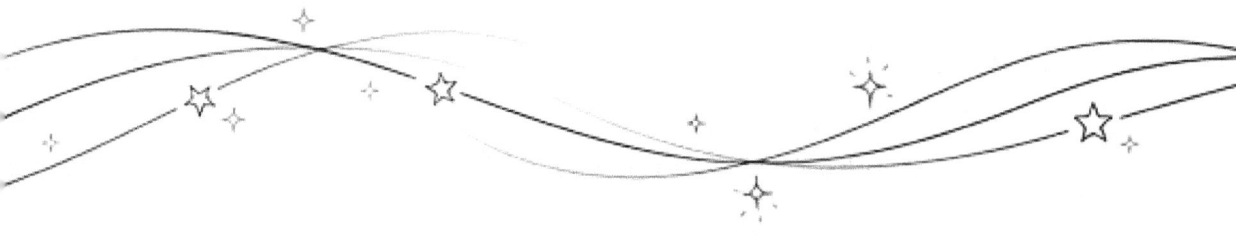

FOUR
Worth Beyond Your Position

Starter, benched, injured, cut from the lineup;

your value doesn't move with your minutes.

So the last will be first, and the first will be last.

— **MATTHEW 20:16**

📖 When You're Not Getting the Minutes You Wanted

This one can sting, so I'm just going to say it plainly:

> Getting benched hurts.

Not always because you want attention (though yes, you want to play, obviously). It hurts because it can feel like being less than. Like you're invisible. Like your effort didn't matter. Like everyone's watching you sit there trying to look fine when you're not fine.

And then your brain starts doing that thing where it turns your situation into your identity:

- "I'm not good enough."
- "Coach doesn't believe in me."
- "I'm falling behind."
- "Everyone else is improving and I'm stuck."
- "If I mattered, I'd be out there."

But here's a truth that will save you (and your confidence) over and over again:

Your position is not your value.

Not your spot on the field.
Not your number of minutes.
Not your ranking.
Not your role.

Jesus said, *"The last will be first."* That's not Him being confusing on purpose. It's Him flipping the way the world measures worth.

The world says:
More playing time = more important.

Jesus says:
I see hearts. I see faithfulness. I see the unseen.

Sometimes you're in a season where you're playing a lot. Sometimes you're in a season where you're learning. Sometimes you're in a season where you're rebuilding after an injury. Sometimes you're in a season where you're being shaped.

And yes, your feelings are valid. It's okay to be disappointed, and you don't have to pretend it doesn't hurt. But you don't get to decide you're worthless because your role feels smaller right now.

A smaller role doesn't mean a smaller life. It might mean God is building something in you that won't break the moment you're finally in the spotlight.

This week, your mission is to hold this line:

My worth is steady. My season can change.

🎯 GAME-DAY MINDSET: CONTROL WHAT YOU CAN CONTROL

You can't always control:

- your coach's decisions
- the lineup
- other people's opinions
- who gets noticed

But you *can* control:

- your effort
- your attitude
- your preparation
- your character
- how you respond when it's hard

This week's cue phrase:

☑ **"I matter, even here."**

Say it when you're waiting. Say it when you're overlooked. Say it when you feel the temptation to shut down. Because showing up with a good attitude when you're disappointed? That's next-level strength.

🏋️ Training Room Application: The Bench to Builder Plan

If you're benched, limited, or waiting your turn, don't waste the moment—use it.

Pick one builder habit for the week:

1. **Eyes-on learning:** Watch the game like a student.
   - What patterns do you notice?
   - What decision-making is winning plays?
2. **Energy teammate:** Choose to be someone's boost.
   - High fives. Encouragement. Positive talk.
   - Not fake, just steady.
3. **Skill focus:** Choose one skill to sharpen quietly.
   - Footwork, passing, shooting, endurance, flexibility…whatever fits your sport.
4. **Coachability move:** Ask one simple question after practice:
5. "Coach, what's one thing I can work on this week?"

That question is so powerful. It shows maturity, and it gives you direction instead of guessing.

Mindset Reps Journal Time

What emotions come up for me when I'm benched, limited, or not chosen? (Name them honestly.)

What story do I start believing about myself in those moments?

What's a healthier truth I can replace that story with? Write it like a statement I can repeat.

What is one thing I can learn by watching instead of playing (strategy, positioning, communication)?

If God is growing something in me in this season, what might it be?

_____
_____
_____
_____
_____
_____
_____
_____
_____
_____
_____
_____

🙏 Prayer

God, You see me when I feel overlooked.

You see my effort, my disappointment, and the parts no one claps for.

Help me remember that my worth doesn't rise and fall with my role.

Give me patience, maturity, and courage to keep showing up.

Teach me to be faithful where I am, and to trust You with what's next.

Amen.

🔥 Weekly Challenge: Faithful in the Small

This week, choose **one** moment that feels small or frustrating, such as bench time, limited minutes, being ignored, not getting credit.

In that moment, do this:

1. Whisper: **"I matter, even here."**
2. Do one "builder action": encourage, learn, prepare, or ask for feedback.
3. Afterward, write one sentence:
4. **"Today I showed strength by…"**

Being faithful in the small moments is what builds the kind of athlete (and the kind of woman) who can handle the big ones.

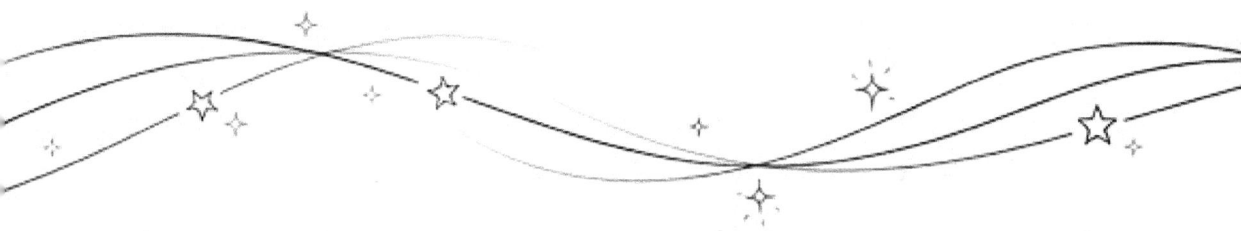

FIVE
The Enough Mindset

You are not behind.

You are not less.

You are not missing something.

You are enough in God's eyes.

I praise You because I am fearfully and wonderfully made.

— **PSALM 139:14**

📖 When Comparison Gets Loud

Comparison is sneaky, and it can ruin your mood in about three seconds. You can be feeling totally fine, then you see someone's highlight video, a photo dump, a new PR post, or a teammate casually saying, "Ugh I played so bad," after scoring three goals.

And your brain goes:

> Cool, so I'm basically the weakest link. *Awesome.*

However, comparison doesn't just steal joy; it messes with your identity. Suddenly you're not thinking, "Why am I not her?"

And the worst part is this: comparison is never fair. You're comparing your behind the scenes to someone else's best angle, best lighting, best moment, best day. Here's what Psalm 139:14 is saying to you, straight up:

> God designed you on purpose. Not accidentally.
> Not as a "less good" version of someone else.

That means there is no such thing as "God made a mistake with me." So, when your mind starts listing everything you do not have, do not look like, or cannot do yet, you need a new script. A truer one. Because being "enough" doesn't mean you never improve. It means you stop treating improvement like proof you are worthy. You can want growth without hating where you are right now.

This week, your goal is not to stop noticing other people. That is impossible. Your goal is to stop letting other people decide how you feel about yourself.

You have your own lane.
You have your own pace.
You have your own calling.

And God is not asking you to be anyone else.

🎯 GAME-DAY MINDSET: STAY IN YOUR LANE

When you compare, you drift. You lose focus. You play tight. You overthink. You forget what you are good at.

Staying in your lane looks like this:

- I celebrate others without shrinking myself.
- I learn from others without copying them.
- I compete with my past self, not someone else's highlight reel.

THIS WEEK'S CUE PHRASE:

☑ **"I'm growing. I'm enough."**

Say it when you feel the comparison spiral start.

🏋️ TRAINING ROOM APPLICATION: THE COMPARISON DETOX

Try this for one week. Yes, one week. You can do hard things.

1. **Unfollow or mute one account that triggers comparison.** Not because they are bad, but simply because your peace matters.
2. **Limit highlight watching before practice or games.** If it makes you feel pressured, it's not helping.
3. **Create a "Wins List" on your phone.** Add 3 wins after every practice. They don't have to be big.
    - "I stayed calm after a mistake."
    - "I tried a new skill."
    - "I encouraged someone."
    - "I showed up even when I was tired."
4. **Choose one growth goal that is yours.** Not your coach's favourite. Not your teammate's thing. Yours.

Mindset Reps Journal Time

- What triggers my comparison the most (social media, certain teammates, certain situations)?

- When I compare, what do I start believing about myself?

- Write a truth statement based on Psalm 139:14 that you want to believe this week.

- What is one area where I have grown in the last 3 months, even a little?

- What is one goal I want to pursue for me, not to "keep up" with someone else?

_____
_____
_____
_____
_____
_____
_____
_____
_____
_____
_____
_____

🙏 Prayer

God, help me stop measuring myself against everyone around me.

Thank You for creating me with purpose and care.

When comparison gets loud, remind me of what is true.

Teach me to celebrate others without shrinking myself.

Help me grow with peace, and to see myself the way You see me.

Amen.

🔥 Weekly Challenge: Wins Over Comparison

For the next 7 days:

1. Each time you catch yourself comparing, whisper: **"I'm growing. I'm enough."**
2. Write down **one win** that has nothing to do with being better than someone else.
3. At the end of the week, read your wins list out loud.

Build a mindset that doesn't fall apart every time someone else shines; it's a solid power move.

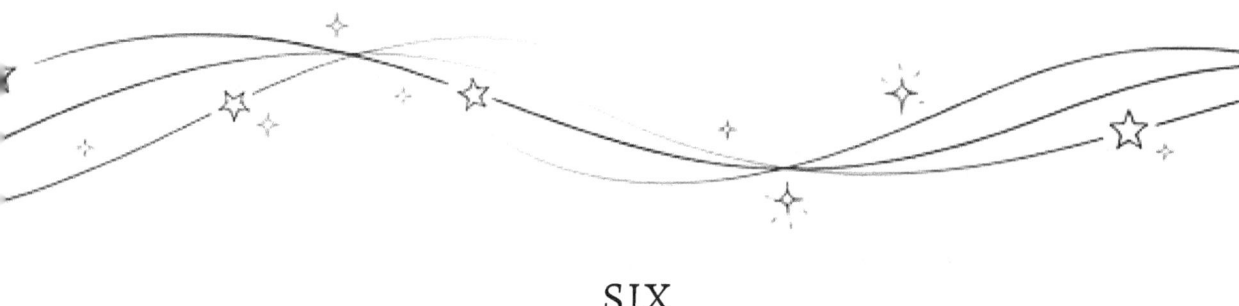

SIX
Faith That Shows Up to Practice

Faith is not just something you feel.

It is something you live, even on ordinary days.

Faith by itself, if it is not accompanied by action, is dead.

— **JAMES 2:17**

📖 The Power of the Ordinary

A lot of people picture faith as this big, emotional moment. Like you are standing on a mountain at sunrise with worship music playing, having a life-changing spiritual breakthrough. But real faith usually looks... normal.

It looks like showing up when you do not feel like it.

It looks like doing the drill again.

It looks like running the extra rep when no one is watching.

It looks like being kind when you are in a mood.

It looks like choosing discipline over drama.

James 2:17 is not trying to make you feel guilty, but to remind you of your boundless strength. Faith is not only what you believe in your head. Faith becomes real when it shows up in your choices.

It's easy to say "I trust God" when you are winning. It's harder to trust God when you are frustrated, tired, or feeling behind. It's also easy to post a verse, but it's harder to live it when your teammate annoys you, your coach corrects you, or your confidence feels shaky.

So, this week, we are focusing on faith that shows up to practice. Not perfect faith. Not loud faith. Not "I have it all together" faith.

Just steady faith. The kind that says:

> *God, I want to honor You today.*
> *Help me do the next right thing.*

That's faith in action, and it changes you over time. Also, can we be real? Most of your life is made of ordinary days. If your faith only works on the big days, it is not strong enough yet. God can meet you in the ordinary, He can shape you in the ordinary, and He can grow you in the ordinary.

So if today feels boring, repetitive, or unglamorous, do not underestimate it. This is where champions are built. This is where character is built. This is where faith becomes real.

🎯 Game-Day Mindset: Effort Is Worship

When you give your best effort, you are not just being a good athlete. You are being faithful.

Not because God only loves you when you work hard.

Because showing up with integrity and effort is a way of honoring Him.

This week's cue phrase:

☑ **"I show up with faith."**

Say it when you feel lazy, distracted, or tempted to coast.

🏋️ Training Room Application: The Faith and Follow-Through Plan

Choose one of these and commit to it for 7 days:

✔ **The 5-Minute Verse Habit**: Read your weekly verse once a day and write one sentence about it.

. . .

✓ **The Effort Upgrade**: Pick one part of practice where you normally coast and choose to give full effort there.

✓ **The Attitude Check**: Before practice, ask God for help with your attitude. After practice, rate it 1 to 10 and write one way to improve tomorrow.

✓ **The Teammate Lift**: Encourage one teammate per practice. Make it specific, not fake.

Remember, tiny actions create real change.

Mindset Reps Journal Time

Where do I tend to "say the right thing" about faith, but struggle to live it out?

What is one ordinary habit that could make me stronger spiritually and mentally?

What is one area of practice where I need more follow-through?

How do I usually act when I am tired or annoyed? What would faith look like in that moment?

Write a short prayer you can say before practice this week. Keep it simple.

_____
_____
_____
_____
_____
_____
_____
_____
_____
_____

🙏 Prayer

God, thank You that You meet me in ordinary days.

Help me live my faith, not just talk about it.

Give me discipline, focus, and a steady heart.

Teach me to show up with effort and integrity, even when no one notices.

Make my actions match what I say I believe.

Amen.

🔥 Weekly Challenge: One Week of Follow-Through

Pick one simple faith action and do it every day for 7 days:

- Read the verse and write one sentence
- Encourage one teammate
- Give full effort in one drill
- Do the attitude check

At the end of the week, write this sentence in your journal:

> **"This week, I learned that faith grows when I…"**

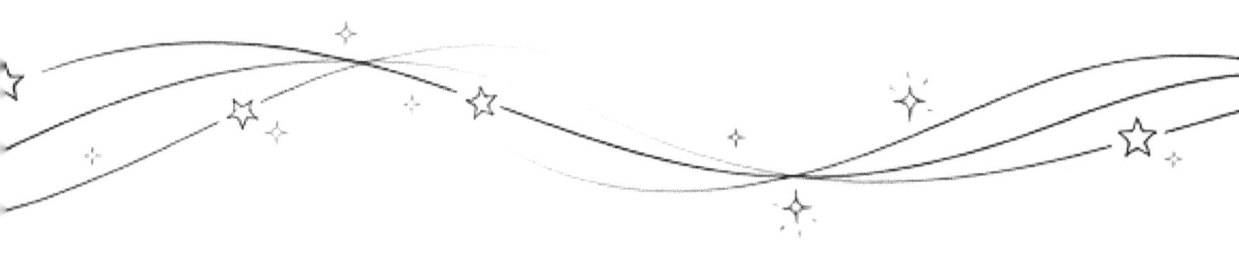

SEVEN
Mind Renewal, Mindset Training

What you repeat in your mind becomes what you believe,
and what you believe affects how you play.

Do not conform to the pattern of this world, but be transformed by the renewing of your mind.

— **ROMANS 12:2**

📖 Your Thoughts Talk All Day

You can be going through the motions of a normal day, sitting in class or warming up for practice, and your brain is basically a full-time commentator.

Sure, sometimes it's helpful:

> "Okay, focus. You've got this."

But it's also sometimes chaotic:

> "You're going to mess up."
> "Everyone is better than you."
> "If you fail, you'll look stupid."
> "Why did you even try?"

The problem is that your brain will say things that are not true with a lot of confidence. And if you keep hearing the same negative thoughts on repeat, they start to feel like facts.

Romans 12:2 says you can be transformed by renewing your mind. That means you can change what runs your life, not by becoming a totally different person overnight, but by changing what you feed your mind and what you agree with.

Think of it like training. You don't build strength with one workout; you build it with repetition. Mindset works the same way. Confidence does not just appear. It is built.

Peace does not just happen. It is practiced.

This week, we're not trying to stop having negative thoughts, because that's simply unrealistic. You're human, and thoughts will come. What we're doing is something more powerful: We are learning to notice a thought, test it, and replace it.

Know that not every thought deserves a seat at the table. In fact, some thoughts are just fear in a hoodie pretending to be wisdom.

Renewing your mind is learning to say:

*"That thought is loud, but it is not true.
I'm choosing truth."*

And truth is not just positive vibes. Truth is what God says about you.

You are loved.
You are growing.
You are not alone.
You are capable of learning.
You can reset after mistakes.
God is with you.

This week, your goal is to become the kind of athlete who does not get pushed around by her own mind.

🎯 Game-Day Mindset: Catch It, Check It, Change It

Use this simple 3-step tool when your thoughts start spiraling.

1. **Catch it:** What am I telling myself right now?
2. **Check it:** Is this true? Is it helpful? Is it what God would say?
3. **Change it:** Replace it with a truth statement.

This Week's Cue Phrase:

☑ **"I choose truth."**

Say it when your mind starts getting dramatic.

🎯 Training Room Application: The Thought Swap Drill

Pick one negative thought you deal with often. Write it exactly as it shows up.

Examples:

- "I always mess up under pressure."
- "I'm not as good as everyone else."
- "If I make a mistake, my coach will be mad."
- "I'm going to embarrass myself."

Now create your **Truth Swap**.

Examples:

- "I can reset quickly and keep going."
- "I am improving through practice."
- "One mistake does not define me."
- "God is with me, and I can do the next right thing."

Do this daily:

- Read the negative thought once.
- Read the truth swap three times.
- Use it at practice when you feel pressure.

This is literally training your brain.

🌱 Mindset Reps Journal Time

👁️ What is the most common negative thought I hear in my mind during sport?

🔍 Is that thought true, or is it fear pretending to be a fact? Why?

✳️ Write one Truth Swap that I can repeat this week. Make it simple and believable.

📌 When do my thoughts get the loudest, before games, during mistakes, after criticism?

📖 Write Romans 12:2 in your own words. What does "renewing my mind" looks like for me?

_____
_____
_____
_____
_____
_____
_____
_____
_____
_____
_____
_____

🙏 Prayer

God, my mind gets loud sometimes.

Help me notice the thoughts that are hurting me.

Teach me to replace fear with truth.

Renew my mind and make me steady under pressure.

Help me choose what You say about me over what my anxiety says.

Amen.

🔥 Weekly Challenge: 7-Day Truth

For the next 7 days:

1. Pick one Truth Swap statement.
2. Say it every day before practice or school.
3. Each time you catch a negative thought, whisper: **"I choose truth."**
4. At the end of the week, write:

> **"The biggest change I noticed in my mindset was…"**

You can't control every thought that shows up, but you *can* control which thoughts you build your life on.

EIGHT
Courage to Be Seen Trying

Courage is not being fearless.

Courage is doing it while your heart is pounding.

Be strong and courageous… for the Lord your God will be with you wherever you go.

— **JOSHUA 1:9**

📖 The Fear of Looking Dumb

If there is one fear that quietly runs a lot of teen athletes, it is this:

What if I look stupid?

Not just "what if I lose."

More like:

- What if I mess up in front of everyone?
- What if I try something new and fail?
- What if people laugh?
- What if my teammates judge me?
- What if my coach thinks I'm not good?

That fear can make you play small.
You stop taking risks.
You stop asking questions.
You stop trying new skills.
You play safe and stay predictable.
And then you wonder why you feel stuck.

Here's the truth. Every athlete you admire got good by being willing to look bad at first.

No one is instantly confident at a new move.

No one learns fast without failing a few times.

No one becomes brave by avoiding the scary thing.

Joshua 1:9 is not a "be tough" speech. It is God saying:

> *You are not doing this alone. I am with you.*

Courage is not pretending you are fine. Courage is choosing to show up even when you are nervous, even when you might mess up, even when people might notice.

This week, God is inviting you to stop hiding your effort. Because effort is not embarrassing, trying is not cringe, and learning is not weakness. The only thing that keeps you stuck is refusing to be seen trying.

You were made to grow.
You were made to stretch.

You were made to become stronger than your fear.

🎯 Game-Day Mindset: Bravery Is a Choice

Courage isn't a personality type, it's a decision. You don't wait to feel brave, you choose brave actions, and the feelings catch up later.

This week's cue phrase:

☑ **"I can be brave."**

Say it right before you do the thing you want to avoid.

🏋 Training Room Application: The Brave Rep Plan

Pick one brave thing to do this week:

1. **Try a new skill** you have been avoiding.
2. **Ask your coach a question** instead of staying silent.
3. **Speak up** with a teammate, kindly but clearly.
4. **Go harder in a drill** even if you might mess up.

5. **Join in** instead of hanging back.

Now make it measurable:

- I will do one Brave Rep each practice this week.
- I will ask one question by Friday.
- I will attempt the new move three times this week.

Bravery grows with reps, just like anything else.

🍃 Mindset Reps Journal Time

☺ What am I afraid will happen if I mess up in front of others?

💭 What is the worst thing my mind says about me when I fail?

✘ What is one Brave Rep I can commit to this week? Write it as a clear plan.

⚑ Where do I play it safe instead of playing to grow? Why?

🙏 If God is with me wherever I go, what would change about the way I show up?

_____
_____
_____
_____
_____
_____
_____
_____
_____
_____
_____

🙏 Prayer

God, You know what I'm afraid of.

You know when I want to hide or play small.

Help me be strong and courageous, not because I feel fearless, but because You are with me.

Give me the courage to try, to learn, and to keep going even after mistakes.

Teach me to grow through discomfort and to trust You in the process.

Amen.

🔥 Weekly Challenge: Brave Rep

This week, do one Brave Rep at every practice or training session.

When you do it:

1. Whisper: **"I can be brave."**
2. Do the brave action.
3. After practice, write one sentence:

> **"Today I was brave when I…"**

Courage isn't loud, but it is consistent. And you're building it, one rep at a time.

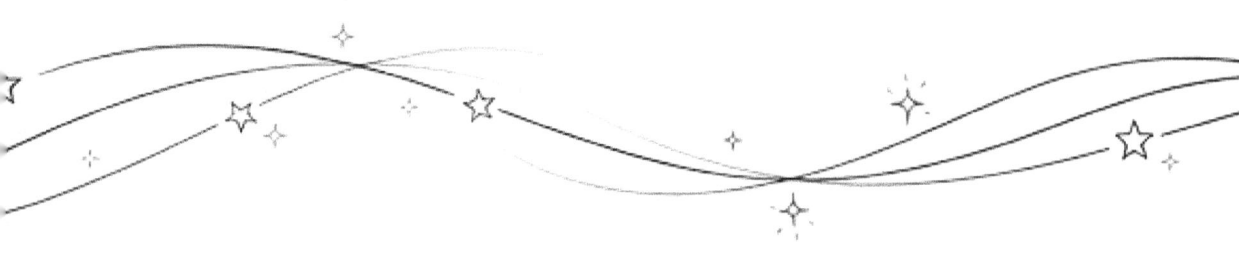

NINE
Praise Without Pressure

Compliments feel good, but they are not your identity.

Let another praise you, and not your own mouth.

— **PROVERBS 27:2**

📖 When Compliments Start Controlling You

Getting praised is nice. Like, genuinely. It feels good when someone notices your effort, your improvement, your leadership, or that one moment you absolutely nailed. In fact, sometimes praise is exactly what you needed to hear. However, the tricky part is that praise can turn into pressure if you start needing it to feel okay.

It can sound like this in your head:

- "I played so well last week, I have to do that again."
- "Now everyone expects me to be amazing."
- "If I have a bad game, I'll disappoint them."
- "What if that was a fluke?"
- "What if I cannot live up to it?"

Praise is like sugar. A little is fun, but too much, and you crash. God doesn't want you trapped in a cycle where your mood depends on what people say about you.

Proverbs 27:2 is not saying compliments are bad. It is saying your life should not be built on applause. Because applause is not steady. People can be excited one day and silent the next. They can hype you up and forget two minutes later.

So, what do you do with praise?

You can receive it without letting it own you.

Here is a healthy way to handle it:

1. **Accept it with gratitude.**
2. **Give credit to God and your effort.**
3. **Stay focused on growth, not maintaining a "perfect image."**

The goal is not to become the girl who is always impressive, but to become the girl who is steady, humble, and confident no matter what the scoreboard says. This week, your win is not chasing more compliments. Your win is staying grounded when you get them.

🎯 Game-Day Mindset: Gratitude, Then Grounding

When someone praises you, try this simple pattern:

- ✔ **Gratitude:** "Thank you, that means a lot."
- ✔ **Grounding:** "I'm just going to keep working."

This will keep your heart humble and your mind calm.

This week's cue phrase:

☑ **"I stay grounded."**

Say it when you feel the pressure of expectations rising.

🏋️ Training Room Application: The Praise Filter

This week, practice filtering praise through truth.

When you get a compliment, do these 3 steps:

1. **Receive it:** Say thank you. Make eye contact. Do not argue.
2. **Remind yourself:** "This is encouragement, not a contract."
3. **Refocus:** Choose one skill to keep improving, even if people think you are already great.

Also, watch your self-talk. Praise can make you secretly scared of failing. If you notice that fear, name it and reset.

Mindset Reps Journal Time

How do I usually react to compliments, do I accept them, brush them off, or feel pressure?

When I get praised, what expectations do I place on myself afterward?

Write a grounding truth I can repeat when praise turns into pressure.

How can I give God credit for my gifts and still take responsibility for my effort?

What is one area I want to keep growing in, even if people already think I'm "good"?

_____
_____
_____
_____
_____
_____
_____
_____
_____
_____
_____

🙏 Prayer

God, thank You for encouragement and the people who notice my effort.

Help me receive praise with gratitude and humility.

Protect my heart from needing applause to feel secure.

Keep me grounded in truth and focused on steady growth.

Teach me to honor You with my attitude, whether I'm noticed or not.

Amen.

🔥 Weekly Challenge: Compliment Without Clinging

This week, when someone compliments you:

1. Say: "Thank you, I appreciate that."
2. Whisper to yourself: "I stay grounded."
3. Write down one sentence later: **"What I'm proud of today is…"**
4. Make it about effort or character, not just performance.

Compliments are lovely, but they are not your foundation. You already have one, and it is stronger.

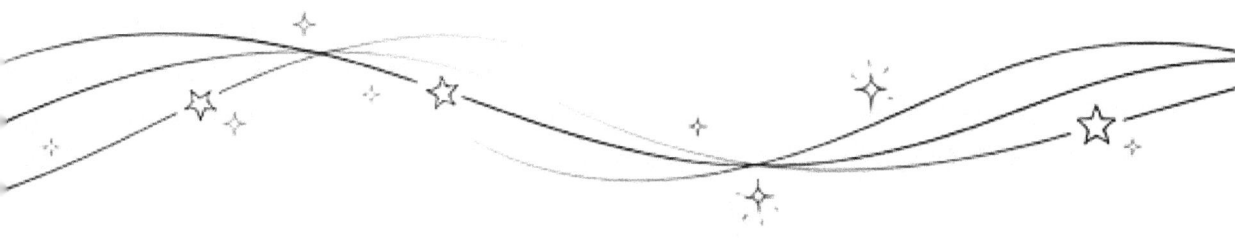

TEN
Criticism Without Crumbling

Feedback can help you grow, but it
does not get to define you.

Whoever heeds life-giving correction will be at home among the wise.

— **PROVERBS 15:31**

📖 When Words Hit Hard

Criticism can feel like getting tagged in a video you did not ask to be in.

Even if the feedback is fair, it can still sting. And if it is unfair, rude, or delivered badly, it can mess with your confidence fast.

Here are a few ways criticism shows up in athlete life:

- A coach corrects you in front of everyone.
- A teammate makes a comment that is "just joking" but does not feel like a joke.
- A parent picks apart the whole game on the ride home.
- Someone online has an opinion they did not earn.
- You hear whispers and suddenly you are overthinking everything.

And then your brain tries to turn one comment into a full identity:

"I'm not good."
"I always mess up."
"They probably regret picking me."
"Everyone thinks I'm annoying."
"I should stop trying."

Proverbs 15:31 calls correction "life-giving." That does not mean it feels nice. It means it can lead to growth when it is handled wisely. This week is about learning a skill that strong athletes have:

How to take feedback without falling apart.

Because there are two unhealthy extremes:

1. **Ignore** all feedback: Keeps you stuck.
2. **Absorb** all feedback: Destroys your confidence.

God is calling you to a middle path, the strong path.

You can listen, learn, and improve without letting criticism become your personal label. A coach can point out a mistake, but that does not mean *you* are a mistake.

🎯 Game-Day Mindset: Filter, Then Build

Use this quick filter when criticism hits:

1. **Is it true?**
2. **Is it useful?**
3. **Is it kind?**

If it's true and useful, keep it. If it's not useful nor kind, do not let it live in your head rent-free.

This week's cue phrase:

☑ **"I can learn and stay steady."**

🏋 Training Room Application: The Feedback Playbook

Try this 3-step response the next time you receive criticism.

1. Pause and breathe
One slow inhale, one slow exhale. This stops the emotional spiral.

2. Respond with maturity
Say one of these:

- "Got it, I'll work on that."
- "Thanks, I'll adjust."
- "Can you show me what you mean?"
- "What should I focus on next time?"

3. Choose one action
Pick one clear adjustment you can do at the next rep, next drill, or next game.

That's how you turn feedback into fuel.

Mindset Reps Journal Time

- What type of criticism hits me the hardest, coach feedback, teammate comments, parents, or social media?

- What do I usually tell myself after criticism? Write it exactly.

- Write a steady truth statement I want to believe instead.

- Think of one piece of feedback I have received recently. What is the useful part I can apply?

- Is there any comment I need to let go of because it is not kind or not useful? What would letting go look like?

_____
_____
_____
_____
_____
_____
_____
_____
_____
_____
_____
_____

🙏 Prayer

God, help me handle feedback with wisdom.

When criticism stings, keep me steady.

Show me what is true and useful so I can grow.

Protect my heart from shame and from believing lies about myself.

Teach me to stay humble, coachable, and confident in You.

Amen.

🔥 Weekly Challenge: One Takeaway

This week, the next time you get criticism or correction:

1. Listen without interrupting.
2. Whisper: **"I can learn and stay steady."**
3. Write down one takeaway only.
4. Just one. Not ten. Not a full self-roast.

Then ask yourself:

What is one thing I can do differently next time?

You're not here to be flawless! You're here to grow, and wise athletes learn how to grow without crumbling.

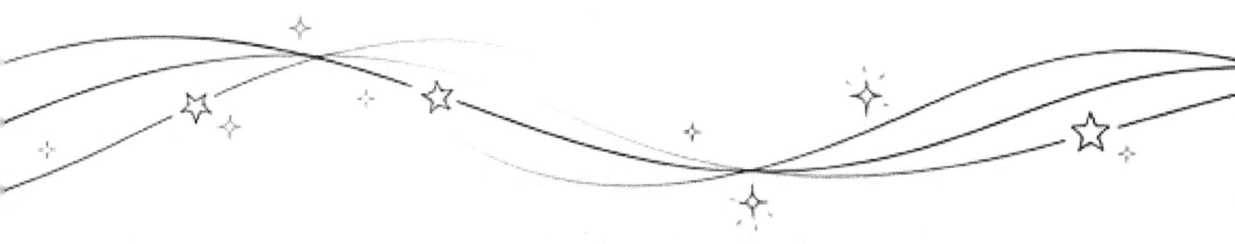

ELEVEN
The Next Play Mentality

What happened happened.

Your power is in what you do next.

Forgetting what is behind and straining toward what is ahead, I press on toward the goal.

— PHILIPPIANS 3:13–14

📖 Getting Unstuck After a Mistake

You know that moment when you mess up, and your body keeps playing but your mind stays behind? Like your brain is still replaying the mistake in slow motion, with dramatic sound effects.

And while you are stuck thinking about what you should have done, the game is still happening. Which usually leads to another mistake. Then another.

Then the spiral starts.

A lot of athletes do not struggle with talent; they struggle with recovery time. Not physical recovery, but mental recovery. While some people bounce back fast, others carry one mistake for the rest of the game like a heavy backpack.

Here is what Philippians 3:13–14 teaches:

You can learn from the past without living in it.

Paul is not saying, "Pretend nothing happened." He is saying, "Don't get trapped staring backwards." You can't run forward while looking behind you. God wants you to become the kind of athlete who can say:

"Yes, that happened. And I'm still here.
I still have purpose. I still get another chance."

Your mistakes are information, and precious opportunities to learn and grow. So, this week, we are practicing the Next Play mentality. Not because mistakes don't matter, but because you're no longer going to let one moment steal the whole game.

God's grace meets you in the reset.

🎯 Game-Day Mindset: The Reset Is a Skill

The Next Play mentality is not a personality trait. It's a practice.

THE NEXT PLAY MENTALITY

Here's a simple rule:

Regret is not a strategy. You can acknowledge a mistake quickly, then move on.

THIS WEEK'S CUE PHRASE:
☑ **"Next play."**

Short. Sharp. Effective.

🏋 TRAINING ROOM APPLICATION: THE 3-STEP RESET

Use this right after a mistake, a bad rep, or a tough moment.

1. **Release**
2. Exhale once. Drop your shoulders.
3. **Refocus**
4. Say in your head: **"Next play."**
5. **Re-engage**
6. Pick one simple action:

   - "Sprint back."
   - "Hands up."
   - "Strong pass."
   - "Talk on defense."
   - "Follow through."

This is how you take your mind out of the past and put it back in the moment.

Bonus tip: If you can, **use a physical cue**, like tapping your wristband or adjusting your ponytail. Your body learns faster with a signal.

📝 Mindset Reps Journal Time

🔄 What mistake do I replay the most in my head? Why do I think it sticks?

💭 What usually happens to my performance after I make one mistake?

🧩 What is a simple action cue I can use as my "re-engage" step?

🙏 How do I think God wants me to respond when I mess up? What truth do I need to remember?

✨ Write about a time I bounced back well. What did I do that helped?

_____
_____
_____
_____
_____
_____
_____
_____
_____
_____

🙏 Prayer

God, help me stop living in my mistakes.

Teach me how to reset quickly and play the next moment with confidence.

Remind me that one mistake does not define me.

Give me focus, peace, and the courage to keep going.

Help me press on toward what is ahead.

Amen.

🔥 Weekly Challenge: The Next Play

This week, every time you mess up in practice or a game:

1. Exhale and drop your shoulders.
2. Say: **"Next play."**
3. Do your re-engage action immediately.

After practice, write one sentence:

"Today, I reset when…"

You're building mental toughness that shows up when it matters, and that's a serious advantage.

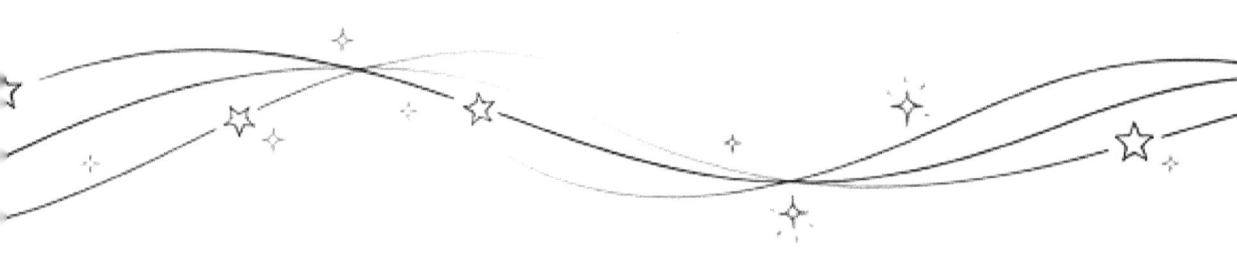

TWELVE
Joy Is Strength

Joy is not something you earn after you win.

Joy is something you choose while you grow.

The joy of the Lord is your strength.

— **NEHEMIAH 8:10**

📖 When Sport Stops Being Fun

Sometimes sport gets heavy. What used to feel fun starts to feel like pressure. What used to feel exciting starts to feel like expectations. You start thinking more about not messing up than enjoying the game.

And joy gets replaced with things like:

- stress
- fear
- comparison
- constant self-criticism
- the feeling that you have to prove yourself

> Here's what Nehemiah 8:10 says:
> **Joy is strength.**

Joy is deeper than a good mood. Joy is steady, and it can exist even when things are hard. Joy is what keeps you going when confidence wobbles.

Joy gives you resilience.

Joy helps you breathe again.

Joy reminds you why you started.

And here is the important part: joy is not the same as taking things lightly. You can take your sport seriously without taking yourself so seriously that you forget how to smile.

God does not want you trapped in a cycle where your sport steals your peace. He gave you gifts, yes, but He also gave you life. And He cares about your heart, not just your performance. Sometimes, the bravest thing you can do is bring joy back on purpose.

Not fake joy, but real joy. The kind that says:

"I'm grateful I get to do this."
"I'm grateful for my body."
"I'm grateful for my team."
"I'm grateful for the chance to grow."

This week, your mission is to reconnect with joy, because joy makes you stronger.

🎯 Game-Day Mindset: Joy Is a Choice You Practice

Joy is not waiting for the perfect game. Joy is choosing gratitude, playfulness, and perspective.

This week's cue phrase:
☑ **"I play with joy."**

Use it when you feel tight, serious, or overwhelmed.

🏋️ Training Room Application: The Joy Reset

Pick one Joy Reset to use at every practice this week:

1. **Smile on purpose** during warm-up. It signals safety to your nervous system.
2. **Gratitude check**: Before practice, name 1 thing you are grateful for about your sport.
3. **Joy playlist**: Listen to one upbeat song before training to shift your mood.
4. **Fun teammate moment**: Give one genuine compliment or joke with someone. Keep it kind.

5. **Breathe and release**: When you feel pressure, take one slow breath and loosen your shoulders.

None of these are magical. They are just ways to remind your mind and body:

"I'm safe. I can enjoy this, and I can play free."

Mindset Reps Journal Time

- When does sport feel the least fun for me, and why?

- What used to bring me joy about my sport when I first started?

- Write 3 things I'm grateful for about my body, my team, or my opportunity to play.

- What steals my joy the fastest (comparison, pressure, criticism, fear)?

- What is one small way I can bring joy into practice this week?

_____
_____
_____
_____
_____
_____
_____
_____
_____
_____

🙏 Prayer

God, thank You for the gift of my sport.

When pressure steals my joy, help me come back to what matters.

Fill me with Your joy, the kind that gives strength and steadiness.

Help me play with gratitude, courage, and freedom.

Teach me to enjoy the process of becoming who You are shaping me to be.

Amen.

🔥 Weekly Challenge: Finding Joy

This week, after each practice or game, write down:

"One moment I enjoyed..."

It can be small, like a good pass, a laugh with a teammate, a strong effort, or even just showing up.

At the end of the week, read your list and remember:

You're allowed to enjoy your life while you grow. Joy is not a distraction; it is strength.

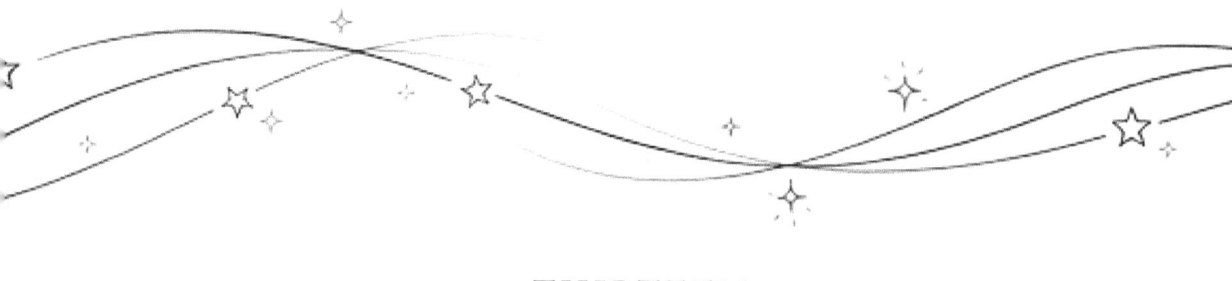

THIRTEEN
Compete With Clean Motives

Your *why* matters.

You can play hard and still keep your
heart at peace.

Create in me a clean heart, O God, and renew a right spirit within me.

— **PSALM 51:10**

📖 What's Really Driving Me?

You can love your sport and still have mixed motives.

Sometimes you train because you want to grow.

Sometimes you train because you are scared of falling behind.

Sometimes you want to win because you love competition.

Sometimes you want to win because you want to prove something.

And if we're being honest, motives can get messy fast:

- I want people to notice me.
- I want to be better than her.
- I want to shut them up.
- I want to look perfect.
- I want to be the "main character" on my team.

Motives matter because they shape what sport does to your heart. If your motive is growth, sport builds you. If your motive is proving yourself, sport can start to break you. When you're playing to prove your worth, every game feels like a test you cannot fail. That's not freedom. That's pressure.

Psalm 51:10 is a simple, brave prayer:

"God, clean my heart."

That doesn't mean you can never want to win. Winning isn't evil, goals are not wrong, and ambition is not a sin. A clean heart simply means that your sport does not become your identity. It means you want success without needing it to feel okay about yourself. It means you compete hard, but don't hate people who beat you. It means you can be confident without being cruel.

God cares about how you play, but he also cares about who you are becoming while you play.

This week, you are not judging yourself, but **reconnecting with your heart**. A clean motive will protect you, keep you steady, and set you free.

🎯 Game-Day Mindset: Compete with Love and Integrity

A clean motive can look like this:

- I play to honor God with my effort.
- I play to grow my skills and character.
- I play to help my team, not just my image.
- I respect opponents because they help me get better.
- I want to win, but I will not lose myself trying.

This week's cue phrase:

☑ "I play with a clean heart."

Use it when you feel jealousy, bitterness, or the urge to prove yourself.

🏋️ Training Room Application: The Motive Check

Do this before practice or a game, once a week.

1. Ask yourself: Why do I want to do well today?
2. Notice what comes up first. No pretending.
3. Pray: "God, clean my heart and renew my spirit."
4. Choose one clean focus for the day:

- effort
- teamwork
- courage
- discipline
- joy
- integrity

This will keep you grounded and help you play from a healthy place.

Mindset Reps Journal Time

- What usually motivates me most, growth, fun, competition, approval, fear, or proving myself?

- What does a "clean heart" in sport look like for me, specifically?

- When do I feel jealousy or comparison on my team? What is underneath it?

- How do I treat teammates or opponents when I feel threatened? What do I want to do differently?

- Write your own one-sentence prayer asking God to renew your spirit in sport.

_____
_____
_____
_____
_____
_____
_____
_____
_____
_____
_____

🙏 Prayer

God, thank You for my sport and the gifts You've given me.

Please create in me a clean heart.

If I am chasing approval, comparison, or pride, help me let it go.

Renew my spirit so I can compete with joy, integrity, and love.

Help me play hard without losing my peace.

Amen.

🔥 Weekly Challenge: Clean Motive, One Choice

This week, choose one "clean heart" action during practice or a game:

- Encourage a teammate who is struggling.
- Show respect to an opponent, even if it's intense.
- Pray quietly before you compete.
- Focus on effort, not attention.
- Celebrate someone else's win without shrinking yourself.

Afterward, write one sentence:

"Today I competed with a clean heart
when I..."

Skills matter.

Winning matters.

But **your heart matters most**, and God is shaping it beautifully.

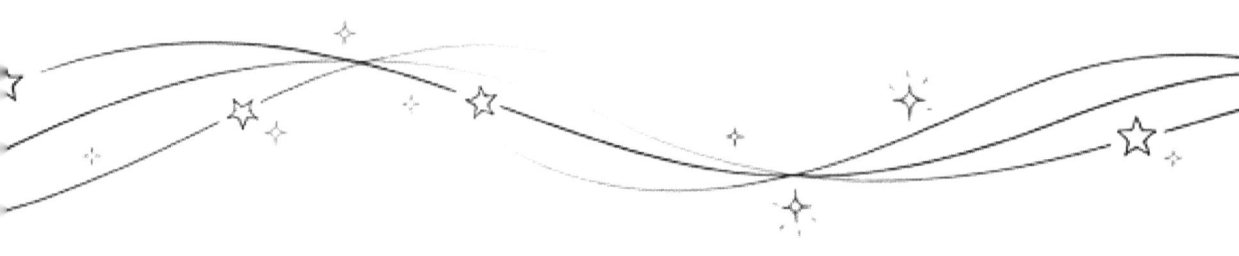

FOURTEEN
Small Habits, Big Results

Tiny choices done consistently shape strong athletes and steady faith.

Do not despise these small beginnings, for the Lord rejoices to see the work begin.

— **ZECHARIAH 4:10**

📖 The Boring Stuff That Builds Champions

Most people want the glow-up without the grind.

They want confidence without repetition, the skill without the awkward learning stage, and the results without the boring basics. But you already know something important: the best athletes are not built on random great days.

They are built on habits.

The weird thing about habits is that they look small in the moment.

One extra stretch.
One extra water bottle.
One extra rep.
One kind choice.
One decision to sleep instead of scrolling.

None of it feels dramatic, but over time, those little choices stack up like bricks. And suddenly you have something strong.

Zechariah 4:10 says God does not roll His eyes at small beginnings. He rejoices to see the work begin.

That means God is not only interested in your big moments. He cares about the day-to-day choices no one claps for. The quiet discipline. The small yes. The "I'll do it anyway."

This week is about getting free from the mindset that says: "If it's not huge, it doesn't matter."

Small habits really matter. They are how you become the kind of athlete who can handle pressure, who improves steadily, who grows in faith without needing constant motivation. You don't need a perfect plan, just a simple one that you can repeat.

🎯 GAME-DAY MINDSET: CONSISTENCY BEATS INTENSITY

A burst of intensity once in a while feels impressive, but consistency changes your life.

THIS WEEK'S CUE PHRASE:

✅ **"Small steps, strong results."**

Use it when you feel tempted to skip the basics or give up because progress feels slow.

🏋️ TRAINING ROOM APPLICATION: PICK YOUR ONE HABIT

Choose **one** small habit for this week. Make it realistic and trackable.

- **Hydration Habit:** Drink a full bottle of water before school ends.
- **Sleep Habit:** Lights out 20 minutes earlier than usual.
- **Mobility Habit:** 5 minutes of stretching after practice.
- **Skill Habit:** 10 minutes on one skill, three times this week.
- **Faith Habit:** Read the weekly verse once a day and write one line about it.
- **Mindset Habit:** Replace one negative thought with one Truth Swap daily.

Now track it. Use a notes app or draw 7 boxes and tick them off. Simple is the secret!

Mindset Reps Journal Time

What small habit would help me most right now in sport, school, or my mindset?

What usually stops me from being consistent, boredom, time, mood, or perfectionism?

What is my One Habit for this week? Write it clearly and make it measurable.

How do I want to feel in 30 days if I stick with small steps?

Ask God for help with consistency. What do I need from Him this week?

_____
_____
_____
_____
_____
_____
_____
_____
_____
_____

🙏 Prayer

God, thank You that You care about the small beginnings.

Help me build habits that make me stronger, healthier, and steadier.

Give me discipline when I feel lazy and patience when progress feels slow.

Teach me to be faithful in the little things.

I want to grow, one small step at a time, with You.

Amen.

🔥 Weekly Challenge: The 7-Day Habit Streak

This week, commit to your One Habit for 7 days.

1. Track it daily.
2. If you miss a day, do not quit. Restart the next day.
3. At the end of the week, write:

"The biggest difference I noticed from one small habit was…"

Small habits are not small when they are repeated. They are how you build the athlete you want to become.

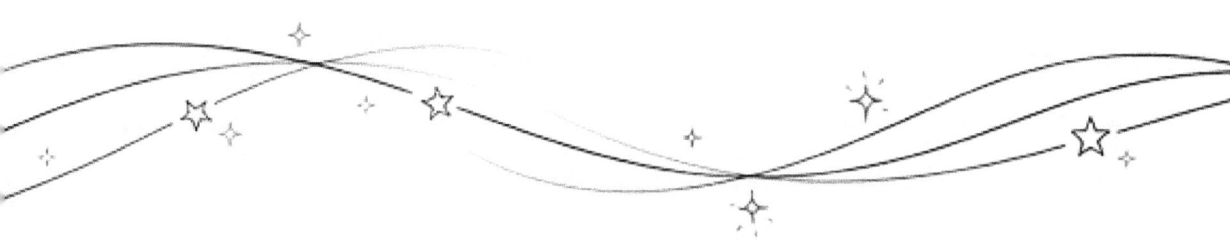

FIFTEEN
Effort Is Your Responsibility

You cannot control everything, but you can control your effort, and God honors that.

Let us not become weary in doing good, for at the proper time we will reap a harvest if we do not give up.

— **GALATIANS 6:9**

📖 THE DAYS YOU DO NOT FEEL LIKE IT

Some days you wake up ready to go. You feel strong, motivated, and locked in. Other days, you feel like a soggy noodle with a schedule.

Those are the days that matter most, because effort is not about your mood. Effort is a choice.

Galatians 6:9 is basically God saying:

> "Do not quit just because it feels slow."

It's so easy to get discouraged when you are not seeing instant results. When you're still not starting, when you still feel nervous, or when your skills are improving, but not as fast as you want. When you are doing the work and it feels like nobody notices.

Here's the truth: effort is not always rewarded immediately, but it is never wasted. Every rep you do while tired builds endurance. Every drill you do when bored builds discipline. Every time you show up with a good attitude, even when you are annoyed, you build character.

Character is what keeps you steady when talent is not enough. God is not asking you to control outcomes. You can't control the scoreboard, the coach, the weather, the referee, or other people's opinions.

But you can control what you bring.

Your effort is your offering.

Not to earn God's love, but to honor Him with the gifts you have.

This week, your goal is to become the athlete who says:

"I might not feel like it, but I will not

quit on myself."

🎯 Game-Day Mindset: Control the Controllables

The controllables are simple:

- effort
- attitude
- preparation
- focus
- communication
- response after mistakes

Everything else is background noise.

This week's cue phrase:

☑ **"My effort is my choice."**

Use it when you feel tempted to coast, complain, or check out.

🏋️ Training Room Application: The Effort Scale

This week, give yourself an effort score after practice.

1. After training, rate your effort from **1 to 10**.
2. Write one reason why you chose that number.
3. Write one small adjustment for tomorrow.

Examples:

- "Today was a 6 because I got distracted and stopped sprinting on transitions."
- "Tomorrow I will focus on finishing every rep strong."

- "Today was an 8 because I worked hard even when I was tired."
- "Tomorrow I will bring better energy at the start."

You're training honesty and discipline at the same time.

🧠 Mindset Reps Journal Time

😔 What usually makes me want to give less effort, tiredness, boredom, stress, fear, or attitude?

🎯 What does "10 out of 10 effort" look like for me, specifically, in my sport?

🌱 Where have I been doing the right things but not seeing results yet? How can I stay patient?

💭 What excuse do I use most often, and what is a stronger replacement thought?

🙏 Write a short prayer for the days I feel weary.

_____
_____
_____
_____
_____
_____
_____
_____
_____
_____
_____
_____

🙏 Prayer

God, help me not grow weary in doing good.

When I feel tired, discouraged, or unmotivated, strengthen me.

Teach me to show up with effort and integrity.

Help me trust that You see the work I do, even when progress feels slow.

Give me endurance and the courage to keep going.

Amen.

🔥 Weekly Challenge: No Coasting

This week, choose **one** part of practice where you tend to coast. Maybe it is conditioning, warm-ups, defense, or the last ten minutes.

Make a plan:

1. Decide the part you will not coast in.
2. Before practice, say: **"My effort is my choice."**
3. Go full effort in that section, every session this week.
4. Afterward, write one sentence: **"Today I chose effort when…"**

Motivation is nice, but effort is powerful. And you are building the kind of strength that lasts.

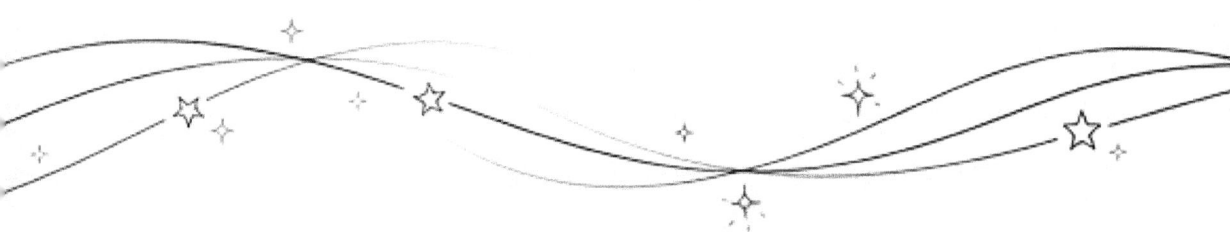

SIXTEEN

Self-Control in the Moment

You cannot control everything around you, but you can control what you do next.

For God gave us a spirit not of fear but of power and love and self-control.

— **2 TIMOTHY 1:7**

📖 When Your Emotions Want to Drive

Athlete life comes with moments that test you fast.

A bad call.
A teammate's comment.
A coach's tone.
A mistake you cannot believe you made.
Someone trash-talking.
A parent yelling from the sideline.

And in those moments, your emotions show up like:

"Say something back."
"Storm off."
"Shut down."
"Prove them wrong."
"Get even."

Here's the problem: emotions are real, but they are not always wise. 2 Timothy 1:7 says God gives you power, love, and self-control. That means self-control is not just "being a good girl." It is spiritual strength. It is leadership. It is maturity. Self-control is what keeps one moment from ruining the whole game.

It is what helps you respond instead of react.

It is what protects your confidence from being hijacked.

It is what keeps your mouth from saying something you regret.

It is what keeps your attitude from turning toxic.

And yes, self-control is harder when you are tired, stressed, hungry, or overwhelmed, so be gentle with yourself. But also, do not excuse yourself. God is shaping you into someone strong enough to stay steady under pressure.

This week is about building the skill of self-control. Not by pretending you never feel big emotions, but by learning how to pause, breathe, and choose.

🎯 Game-Day Mindset: Pause, Then Choose

Self-control is a tiny pause that changes everything.

This week's cue phrase:

☑ **"I choose my response."**

Say it when you feel your emotions rising.

🏋️ Training Room Application: The 5-Second Pause

Try this the next time you are triggered.

1. **Pause for 5 seconds**
2. Count in your head: 5…4…3…2…1…
3. **Exhale slowly**
4. Longer exhale than inhale.
5. **Ask one question:** "What response makes me proud later?"
6. **Choose one calm action:**

- Walk away for a minute
- Take a sip of water
- Ask for clarification instead of snapping
- Say, "Okay," and move on
- Focus on the next rep

Mindset Reps Journal Time

- What situations trigger me the fastest in sport?

- What is my most common reaction when I'm frustrated, snapping, shutting down, getting sarcastic, or giving up?

- What would a self-controlled response look like in that same moment?

- How can I show power and love at the same time when things get tense?

- Ask God for help in one specific area where you need more self-control.

_____
_____
_____
_____
_____
_____
_____
_____
_____
_____
_____
_____

🙏 PRAYER

God, help me stay steady when my emotions feel big.

Thank You that You have given me a spirit of power, love, and self-control.

Help me pause before I react.

Help me choose responses that reflect Your strength in me.

When I'm frustrated, give me calm.

When I'm tempted to snap, give me wisdom.

Amen.

🔥 WEEKLY CHALLENGE: ONE PAUSE

This week, choose one trigger you want to handle better.

When it happens:

1. Do the 5-second pause.
2. Breathe out slowly.
3. Say: **"I choose my response."**
4. Choose a calm action.

After practice or the game, write one sentence:

"Today I showed self-control when…"

Self-control isn't about being perfect, but about becoming powerful in the moments that matter.

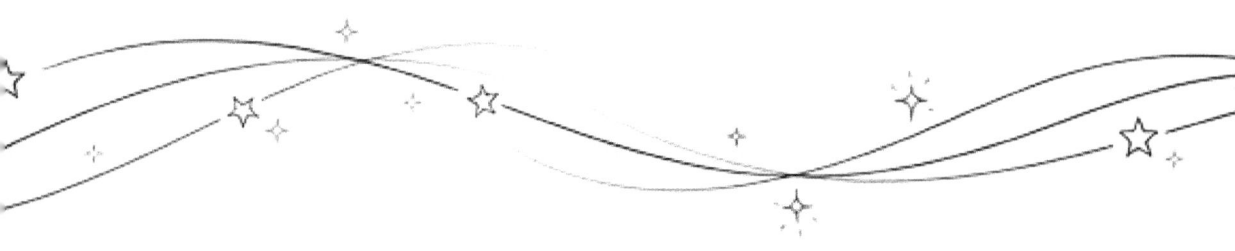

SEVENTEEN
Doing Hard Things on Purpose

Discipline is choosing what matters most, even when it feels uncomfortable.

Do you not know that in a race all the runners run, but only one gets the prize? Run in such a way as to get the prize.

—1 CORINTHIANS 9:24

📖 The Moment You Want to Quit

Every athlete has a moment like this:

> You're tired.
> You're annoyed.
> Your legs feel heavy.
> You're not in the mood.
> You just want to stop.

It might happen during conditioning. It might happen in the middle of a tough drill. It might happen when you are injured and rehab is slow. It might happen when you feel behind and you think, "What's the point?"

That moment is not proof you are weak, but a doorway to becoming strong. 1 Corinthians 9:24 is not about "being the best person ever." It is about intentional effort. It is about running with purpose instead of drifting through life.

Doing hard things on purpose is how athletes are built, and it's also how faith grows. Remember that discipline is both a sport skill and a life skill.

Discipline says:

"I will keep going even when my feelings are loud."

"I will do the right thing even when it is uncomfortable."

"I will not quit just because it is hard."

And Girl, discipline doesn't mean to never rest. Rest is wise, and rest is important. But quitting in the moment because it feels uncomfortable is different.

This week is about **building grit**. The steady kind of grit, the one that helps you push through when you want to give up.

. . .

You absolutely do not have to be perfect. You just have to keep showing up! God is building something in you when you choose the hard thing.

🎯 Game-Day Mindset: Discomfort Is Not Danger

A lot of the time, your body and brain treat discomfort like an emergency, but discomfort is often just growth happening.

This week's cue phrase:

☑ **"I can do hard things."**

Say it when you want to stop.

🏋️ Training Room Application: The "Hard Thing" Rep

Pick one hard thing you usually avoid, and commit to it this week:

- Finish conditioning strong
- Hold a plank 20 seconds longer
- Take the tough shots, not just the easy ones
- Practice the skill that frustrates you
- Do your rehab exercises without skipping

Now, make it specific:

- "I will push through the last 2 minutes of conditioning without quitting."
- "I will do my rehab every day this week."
- "I will attempt my weak skill 10 times each practice."

Mindset Reps Journal Time

What is my hardest part of training, conditioning, discipline, rehab, focus, or confidence?

When I want to quit, what thought usually shows up first?

What is a stronger thought I can use instead this week?

What is my "Hard Thing Rep" plan for this week? Make it clear and measurable.

Ask God to strengthen you. What do you need help with most?

_____
_____
_____
_____
_____
_____
_____
_____
_____
_____

🙏 Prayer

God, give me strength for the hard moments.

Help me not quit when things feel uncomfortable.

Teach me discipline that is rooted in purpose, not pressure.

When I feel weak, remind me that You can strengthen me.

Help me run my race with endurance and courage.

Amen.

🔥 Weekly Challenge: Last Rep

This week, choose one moment in every practice that you normally coast or check out.

When you reach it:

1. Say: **"I can do hard things."**
2. Give your best effort for just one more rep.
3. After practice, write one sentence:

"Today I did a hard thing when…"

Grit is not built in the easy parts. It works its magic when you move through the hard ones.

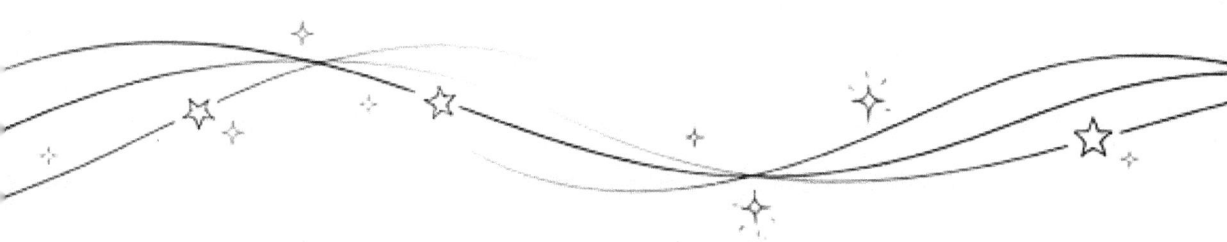

EIGHTEEN
Consistency Over Mood

You will not always feel motivated, but you
can still be faithful and steady.

Blessed is the one... whose delight is in the law of the Lord... That person is like a tree planted by streams of water.

— **PSALM 1:1–3**

📖 When Motivation Disappears

Motivation is a little bit like good lighting. When it shows up, everything feels easier. When it disappears, you're suddenly wondering why you ever thought you could do anything.

Some days, training is exciting. And then there are the days when you feel tired, annoyed, overwhelmed, or just not in the mood. Here is a truth that will help you grow up fast:

Your mood is real, but it is not your boss.

Psalm 1 describes a person who is like a tree planted by streams of water. A tree does not depend on "feeling inspired" to stay alive. It has roots, it is steady, and it stays connected.

That's what consistency does for you: It gives you roots.

Consistency means you show up even when you do not feel like it.

Not with perfection, but certainly with steadiness.

If you only train, pray, read your Bible, or work hard when you feel motivated, your growth will be shaky. God isn't asking you to be intense all the time; he's asking you to be faithful.

Faithfulness looks like:

- showing up to practice with a decent attitude
- doing the basics even when you are bored
- staying connected to God even when you feel distant
- choosing habits that support your goals

This week, you're building steadiness, the kind that makes you strong over time.

🎯 Game-Day Mindset: Roots, Not Waves

When your mood changes, you can still choose your actions.

This week's cue phrase:

☑ **"I show up anyway."**

Say it when you feel tempted to skip, coast, or give up on the day.

🏋 Training Room Application: The Minimum Standard Plan

On low-mood days, you need a simple plan that keeps you consistent without burning you out. Choose a minimum standard for the week. It should be small enough that you can do it even on a tough day.

Examples:

- Show up and complete warm-up and the first 10 minutes fully focused
- Read one verse and write one sentence
- Stretch for 5 minutes after practice
- Drink one full bottle of water before 3 pm
- Get to bed 15 minutes earlier

The goal isn't to do everything, but to stay steady. Remember that consistency is built by keeping promises to yourself, even small ones.

🌱 Mindset Reps Journal Time

- What does a low-mood day look like for me, and what do I usually do?

- What does it mean to have "roots" in my faith and mindset?

- What is my minimum standard for this week? Make it simple and specific.

- What is one excuse I use when I don't feel motivated, and what is a better response?

- How can I stay connected to God even when I don't feel emotionally close?

_____
_____
_____
_____
_____
_____
_____
_____
_____
_____

🙏 Prayer

God, help me be steady.

When my mood is low and motivation is missing, give me strength to show up anyway.

Help me build roots in You so I am not tossed around by feelings.

Teach me faithfulness in small things and consistency in my habits.

Grow me into someone strong and steady over time.

Amen.

🔥 Weekly Challenge: Show Up Anyway

This week, pick one day when you do not feel like training, praying, or doing the right thing.

That day, do your minimum standard.

1. Say: **"I show up anyway."**
2. Do the small commitment.
3. Write one sentence afterward:

> **"Today I was consistent when..."**

Consistency isn't flashy, but it *is* super powerful, and it will take you further than mood ever will.

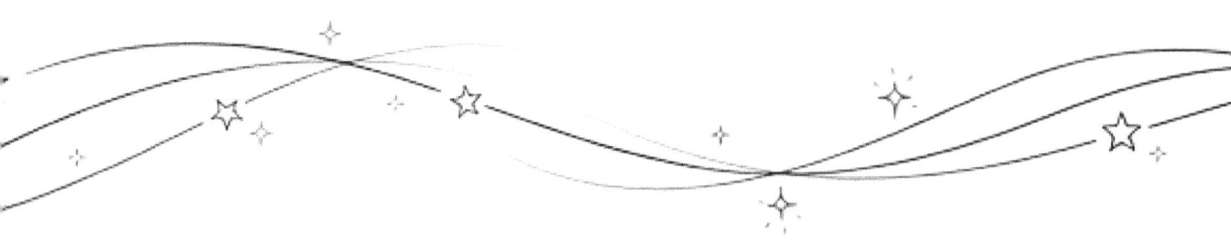

NINETEEN
Focus: One Thing at a Time

You do not have to do everything.

You just have to do the next right thing.

Do not worry about tomorrow, for tomorrow will worry about itself. Each day has enough trouble of its own.

— **MATTHEW 6:34**

📖 When Your Brain Has 37 Tabs Open

Some days the mind can feel like a laptop with way too many tabs open. School. Friends. Sport. Family stuff. Social media. Drama. Homework. Tryouts. Body image. Future plans. That one awkward thing you said three years ago that your brain randomly decides to replay now.

And then you get to practice or a game and you are physically there, but mentally you are everywhere else. That's when focus disappears.

Matthew 6:34 is Jesus telling you something really practical:

Stop living in tomorrow's problems.

Not because tomorrow doesn't matter, but because worrying about it steals your power today. Your mind was not designed to carry everything at once. Focus is a skill, and you can train it. And one of the best ways to train focus is to simplify. You don't need to solve your whole life today. You don't need to be perfect at everything. You don't need to predict every outcome.

You just need to **stay in the moment** you are actually in.

God is here with you. Not just in the future, and not just when things are sorted out. Here, always.

This week, we are practicing one thing at a time.

One drill.
One rep.
One assignment.
One conversation.
One choice.

That's how you get your peace back, and that's how you play free.

🎯 Game-Day Mindset: The Next Right Thing

When you feel overwhelmed, ask yourself:

"What is the next right thing?"

Not the next ten things; just the next **one**.

This Week's Cue Phrase:

☑ **"One thing."**

Say it when your mind starts racing.

🎒 Training Room Application: The Focus Funnel

Use this before practice, games, or even study time.

1. **Brain dump**
2. Write down everything on your mind in 60 seconds. No filter.
3. **Circle what matters right now**
4. Pick one thing you can actually do today.
5. **Choose a focus target**. For practice, it might be:

- communication
- effort on defense
- quick feet
- strong first touch
- breathing and calm resets

Also, **set a short focus window**. Say: "For the next 10 minutes, I'm locked in on this." Short windows make focus possible.

Mindset Reps Journal Time

- What usually distracts me the most during practice or games?

- What are my biggest "tomorrow worries" right now?

- What is one thing I can control today that would help me feel calmer?

- What does focus feel like in my body, and what does distraction feel like?

- Ask God to help you stay present. What do you need to release to Him today?

_____
_____
_____
_____
_____
_____
_____
_____
_____
_____

🙏 Prayer

God, my mind can get overwhelmed and scattered.

Help me stay present and focused on what is in front of me.

Teach me not to worry about tomorrow in a way that steals today.

Give me peace, clarity, and the ability to do the next right thing.

Help me trust You with what I cannot control.

Amen.

🔥 Weekly Challenge: One Thing

This week, before every practice or game:

1. Pick one focus target.
2. Say: **"One thing."**
3. Give your best attention to that one focus for the first 10 minutes.

Afterward, write one sentence:

"Today, my one thing was…, and I noticed…"

It's all about staying faithful to the moment you are in.

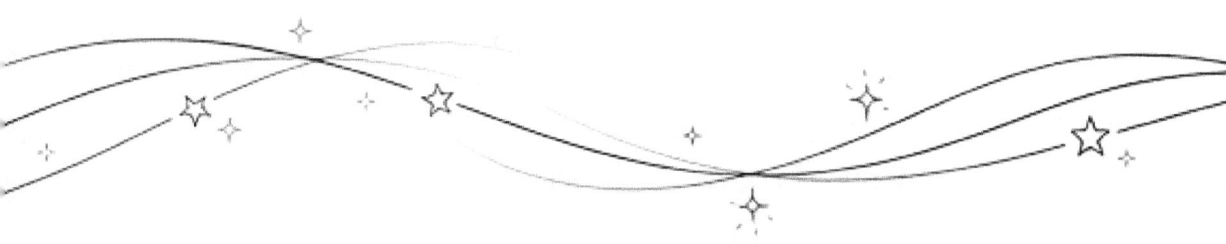

TWENTY

Work Ethic Without Burnout

You can be driven and still be healthy.

Hustle is not the same as purpose.

Come to Me, all you who are weary and burdened, and I will give you rest.

— **MATTHEW 11:28**

📖 When "Trying Hard" Turns into Never Feeling Done

Being a female athlete often comes with a secret pressure: you feel like you have to do more to prove you belong. So you push, you grind, and you stay late. You replay mistakes, and you try to be the hardest worker so nobody can question you.

> Hard work is good. Discipline is good.
>
> Effort matters.

But there is a line where strong work ethic turns into burnout, and it usually sounds like this:

- I can't rest or I'll fall behind.
- If I'm not improving fast, I'm failing.
- I have to be perfect.
- Everyone expects me to be "on" all the time.
- I'm tired, but I should push through anyway.

Matthew 11:28 is Jesus inviting you to something powerful: rest.

> Not quitting. Not laziness.
> **Rest.**

Rest is not a reward for being perfect. It is a requirement for being human. Even machines overheat if they never stop. Your body and brain are not meant to live in constant pressure mode.

Work ethic without rest becomes fear-based. Work ethic with rest becomes sustainable.

. . .

I promise you, God is not impressed by you running yourself into the ground. He cares about your whole life. He cares about your health, your joy, your mind, and your heart.

This week, we are building a balanced work ethic, the kind that says:

> "I will work hard, and I will recover well."
> "I will be disciplined, and I will also be wise."
> "I will train my body, and I will protect my peace."

Strong athletes recover. That's not optional; it's training.

🎯 Game-Day Mindset: Rest Is Part of Training

If you never rest, your performance suffers, your mood suffers, and your faith suffers.

Rest is not weakness. **Rest is strategy**.

This week's cue phrase:
☑ **"Recover to get stronger."**

Use it when you feel guilty for taking a break.

🏋 Training Room Application: The Burnout Check and Reset

This week, do a quick check-in each day.

Rate your tank from 1 to 10: 1 is empty. 10 is energized.

Notice the warning signs:

- you feel irritable all the time
- you dread training
- you are constantly exhausted
- you feel numb or unmotivated
- you cry easily or feel overwhelmed
- your body aches more than usual

Choose one recovery action:

- Go to bed 20 minutes earlier
- Hydrate properly
- Eat a real snack after training
- Put your phone away for 30 minutes
- Take a gentle walk
- Stretch and breathe for 5 minutes
- Pray and release the pressure

Remember that recovery is a daily habit.

📝 Mindset Reps Journal Time

😓 What are my biggest signs that I'm heading toward burnout?

💭 Do I ever feel guilty for resting? Why?

⚖️ What does a healthy work ethic look like for me, not extreme, not lazy, just steady?

🛏️ What is one recovery habit I can commit to this week?

🙏 What do I need to bring to Jesus right now because I feel weary?

_____
_____
_____
_____
_____
_____
_____
_____
_____
_____

🙏 PRAYER

Jesus, I bring You my tiredness and pressure.

Help me work hard with a healthy heart.

Teach me to rest without guilt and recover with wisdom.

Show me where I'm pushing from fear instead of purpose.

Give me peace, strength, and balance.

Help me be a strong athlete with a steady soul.

Amen.

WEEKLY CHALLENGE: RECOVERY

This week, choose **two** recovery actions and do them at least **4 days** this week.

Examples:

- sleep 30 minutes earlier
- no phone 20 minutes before bed
- 5 minutes stretching after training
- drink enough water
- a short prayer reset after practice

At the end of the week, write one sentence:

"When I recovered well, I noticed…"

You don't have to burn out to be dedicated! Choose to be strong and wise at the same time.

TWENTY-ONE
Steward Your Body

Your body is not something to judge.

It is something to care for.

Do you not know that your bodies are temples of the Holy Spirit... Therefore, honor God with your bodies.

— **1 CORINTHIANS 6:19–20**

📖 Your Body Is Not the Enemy

Teen athletes live in a weird world. On one hand, your body is your tool. You train it, push it, rely on it. On the other hand, it is easy to criticize it constantly.

Too slow. Too soft. Too tall. Too short. Too curvy. Not curvy enough. Too muscular. Not toned enough. Why does she look like that and I look like this?

And then there's performance pressure:

"I should be faster."
"I should be stronger."
"I should not get tired."
"I should not need rest."

That's a lot of "should" for one human being. 1 Corinthians 6:19–20 calls your body a temple of the Holy Spirit. That's not about being perfect; it's about value. A temple is cared for, protected, and treated with respect.

Stewardship means you take responsibility for what God has entrusted to you. Your body is a gift, not a project you are allowed to hate until it looks different. And as an athlete, honoring God with your body includes things that are not glamorous:

- eating enough to fuel training
- drinking water
- sleeping
- stretching
- recovering
- speaking kindly about yourself
- getting help when something feels off

It also means you stop punishing your body for being human. God is not asking you to be skinny. He is not asking you to be perfect. He is asking you to honor Him by caring for your body with wisdom and respect.

So this week, we are shifting the question from:

"Do I like how my body looks?"

to:

"How can I take care for my body?"

That's a mindset that builds strength and peace.

🎯 Game-Day Mindset: Fuel, Recover, Respect

Athletes do not just train hard. They recover smart.

Respect for your body looks like:

- fueling it
- listening to it
- training it wisely
- resting it without guilt

This week's cue phrase:
☑ **"My body is a gift."**

Use it when you feel tempted to criticize yourself.

🏋️ Training Room Application: The Body Care Basics

This week, pick **two** of these and do them consistently:

✓ **Hydrate:** drink water before, during, and after training

✓ **Fuel:** eat a real snack within 60 minutes after practice

✓ **Sleep:** aim for an earlier bedtime at least 3 nights

✓ **Stretch:** 5 minutes after training

✓ **Recover:** shower, change, and reset instead of staying sweaty and stressed

✓ **Self-talk:** replace one body-critical thought with a body-respect thought

✓ **Injury wisdom:** if something hurts in a not-normal way, tell someone and get it checked

Small basics will protect your health and performance.

Mindset Reps Journal Time

What is one negative thought I often have about my body?

What is one thing my body allows me to do that I am grateful for?

Do I fuel my body well for training? What is one small improvement I can make this week?

What is one recovery habit I need most right now?

Ask God to help you honor Him with your body. What does that look like for you?

_____
_____
_____
_____
_____
_____
_____
_____
_____
_____
_____

🙏 Prayer

God, thank You for my body and all it does for me.

Help me treat it with respect and care, not criticism and pressure.

Give me wisdom to fuel, rest, and recover well.

Help me listen to my body and speak kindly about myself.

Teach me to honor You with my choices and my mindset.

Amen.

🔥 Weekly Challenge: Body Respect

This week, choose **one** body-respect action to do daily:

- hydrate
- fuel after training
- earlier sleep
- stretch
- kinder self-talk

At the end of the week, write one sentence:

"When I treated my body with respect, I noticed..."

Your body is not your enemy. It is your teammate for life. Treat it like one.

TWENTY-TWO
Preparation Beats Panic

Confidence grows when you prepare.
Panic grows when you procrastinate.

The horse is made ready for the day of battle, but victory rests with the Lord.

— **PROVERBS 21:31**

📖 The Night Before the Big Day

You know that feeling when you have something important coming up and your brain suddenly becomes a dramatic movie trailer?

Tryouts. Finals. A big game. A tough opponent. A new position. A coach watching closely.

Your mind starts throwing all these questions at you: What if I mess up? What if I freeze? What if I disappoint everyone? What if I forget what to do? What if I'm not ready?

Sometimes, what we call nerves is actually a lack of preparation showing up as panic. Not always; some nerves are normal. But preparation gives the mind something steady to stand on.

Proverbs 21:31 says the horse is made ready for battle, but victory rests with the Lord.

This verse is a perfect balance:

- You do your part.
- You trust God with the outcome.

Preparation is doing your part without trying to control everything. It's packing your gear, getting enough sleep, hydrating, reviewing plays, practicing your skills, and calming your mind before the moment.

And here's the best part: Preparation is not just physical, it's spiritual and mental too. When you prepare your mind, you walk into pressure with a plan instead of panic. When you pray, you remember that you are not carrying the whole outcome alone.

. . .

This week, you are learning to trade last-minute stress for **steady readiness**.

🎯 Game-Day Mindset: Do Your Part, Trust God with the Rest

You can control preparation. You cannot control everything else.

This week's cue phrase:
☑ **"Ready and released."**

Ready means you prepared.

Released means you let God carry what you cannot control.

🏋 Training Room Application: The 3-Part Prep Routine

Use this routine before any big day this week.

Practical Prep (5 minutes)

- Pack gear the night before
- Fill your water bottle
- Lay out what you need
- Check times and transport

Mental Prep (2 minutes)

Choose one focus target:

- strong first 5 minutes
- quick reset after mistakes
- communicate loudly

- calm breathing
- aggressive effort

Spiritual Prep (1 minute)

Say a simple prayer:

"God, help me do my part with courage. I trust You with the outcome."

📝 Mindset Reps Journal Time

😨 What situations make me panic the most, games, tryouts, tests, performance, social pressure?

🪞 What does being "prepared" look like for me in those moments?

🧠 What is one mental focus target that helps me feel steady?

🙏 What is one thing I need to release to God because I cannot control it?

☑️ Write a simple prep routine I can follow before a big day. Keep it short.

_____
_____
_____
_____
_____
_____
_____
_____
_____
_____
_____

🙏 Prayer

God, help me prepare with wisdom and not panic with fear.

Teach me to do my part with discipline and confidence.

Help me trust You with the outcome and release what I cannot control.

Give me a calm mind, steady courage, and focus in the moment.

Amen.

🔥 Weekly Challenge: Prep, Then Peace

This week, choose one upcoming pressure moment. It can be a game, a test, or even a hard conversation.

Before it happens:

1. Do your practical prep.
2. Choose one mental focus.
3. Pray and release the outcome.

Afterward, write one sentence:

"Because I prepared, I noticed…"

Preparation isn't about controlling life, but learning to walk into it with steadiness, then trusting God with the rest.

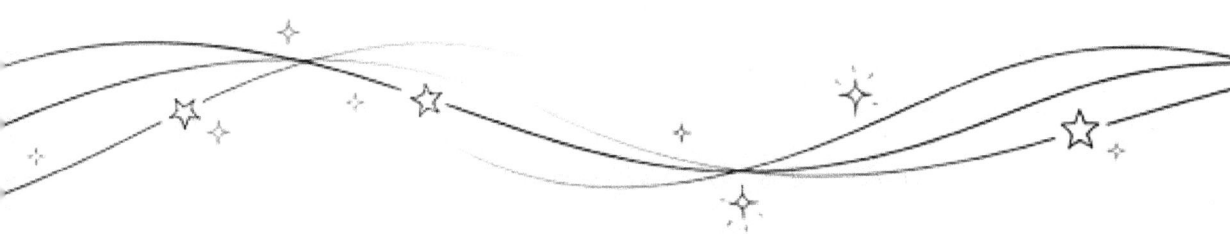

TWENTY-THREE
Train Your Self-Talk

The way you talk to yourself shapes the way you show up.

The tongue has the power of life and death.

— **PROVERBS 18:21**

📖 You Are Always Listening to You

You probably pay attention to what your coach says. You notice what teammates say. You might even replay what someone said in the hallway five hours later.

> But the voice you hear most every day is
> your own.

If your self-talk is harsh, your confidence will feel shaky even when you are improving. Self-talk can sound like:

- "Why am I like this?"
- "I'm so bad."
- "Everyone's watching me."
- "I always mess up."
- "I can't do this."

You might think it is just thoughts. No big deal. But Proverbs 18:21 says words have power of life and death. That includes the words you speak to yourself.

Your brain believes repetition. If you keep repeating the same negative lines, your mind starts treating them like facts. Then you play tighter, you hesitate, you spiral faster, and you stop trying.

Fortunately, self-talk is a skill that you can train. Training your self-talk is not pretending everything is perfect, but choosing words that are true and helpful.

Instead of: "I'm terrible."
Try: "I'm learning. I can adjust."

Instead of: "I always mess up."
Try: "Mistakes happen. I reset quickly."

Instead of: "I can't."
Try: "I can do the next right thing."

God's voice toward you is not cruel. He corrects, but He does not crush. So, if your self-talk sounds like bullying, it is time to change it.

This week, we are replacing life-draining self-talk with **life-giving self-talk**, because you cannot build confidence with a voice that tears you down.

🎯 GAME-DAY MINDSET: SPEAK LIFE UNDER PRESSURE

When pressure rises, your self-talk gets louder, so you need a phrase that is short and steady.

THIS WEEK'S CUE PHRASE:

☑ "I can adjust."

It works for anything: a mistake, a bad start, a tough opponent, a nervous moment.

🏋 TRAINING ROOM APPLICATION: THE SELF-TALK SWAP

This week, choose **one** negative phrase you say often and create a swap for it.

1. Write your most common negative self-talk line.

Examples:

- "I'm so dumb."
- "I'm going to mess up."

- "I'm not good enough."

2. Create a Life-Giving Swap.

Keep it believable:

- "I'm learning and improving."
- "I'm prepared. I can handle this."
- "I belong here."

3. Repeat it on purpose.

Say it:

- before practice
- after mistakes
- during tough drills

Mindset Reps Journal Time

What do I say to myself when I make a mistake?

Which self-talk line drains my confidence the fastest?

Write a Life-Giving Swap that I will practice this week.

How do I play differently when my self-talk is supportive instead of harsh?

Ask God to help you speak life over yourself. What do you need to hear most right now?

_____
_____
_____
_____
_____
_____
_____
_____
_____
_____
_____

🙏 Prayer

God, help me notice when my self-talk is hurting me.

Teach me to speak life, truth, and courage over myself.

Help me replace harsh words with steady, helpful ones.

Remind me that You are patient with me as I learn.

Give me a strong mind and a kind inner voice.

Amen.

🔥 Weekly Challenge: Speak Life

This week, every time you catch harsh self-talk:

1. Pause and notice it.
2. Say: **"I can adjust."**
3. Replace it with your Life-Giving Swap.

After practice, write one sentence:

"Today my self-talk was stronger when…"

You can't always control what happens in a game, but you can control the voice you bring into it. Make it one that builds you up.

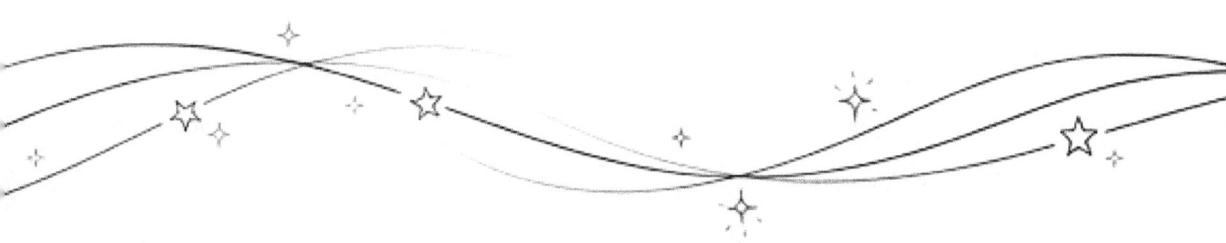

TWENTY-FOUR
Integrity When No One's Watching

Who you are in private shapes who you become in public.

Whoever can be trusted with very little can also be trusted with much.

— **LUKE 16:10**

📖 THE REAL YOU

There are two versions of every athlete: The one people see, and the one you are when nobody is watching. Real growth often happens in the hidden moments:

- when you do the warm-up properly, even if others rush it
- when you return the shopping trolley, even though no one cares
- when you practice your weak skill at home
- when you tell the truth even if lying would be easier
- when you keep your attitude respectful even if you feel annoyed
- when you do the right thing in private

Luke 16:10 says if you can be trusted with little, you can be trusted with much. That means your little moments matter. Integrity is not just about huge moral decisions. It's mostly about small choices that shape your character. Integrity means you do what is right, even when it is inconvenient.

It means that your life matches your values.

It means you do not need to perform goodness for attention.

And for an athlete, integrity also shows up in things like:

- not cutting corners in training
- not blaming others for mistakes
- not gossiping about teammates
- not pretending you did the work when you did not
- not acting one way in front of coaches and another way with teammates

Integrity makes you strong from the inside out.

When your character is steady, your confidence becomes steady too. You do not have to worry about being exposed or found out, because you are the same person in private as you are in public.

This week, God is inviting you to build the kind of character that lasts.

🎯 Game-Day Mindset: Be the Same Person Everywhere

Integrity is being consistent.

This Week's Cue Phrase:

☑ **"I do what's right."**

Say it when you feel tempted to take shortcuts.

🏋 Training Room Application: The Integrity Choice List

Pick two integrity choices to focus on this week:

- Finish warm-ups properly, no half-effort
- Own mistakes quickly without excuses
- Encourage teammates, do not gossip
- Use your phone less before bed so you can recover well
- Do your schoolwork on time, even when you are busy
- Do your extra reps honestly, even if no one checks
- Speak respectfully, even when you disagree
- Spend one minute with God daily, even if you do not feel like it

Remember that small integrity choices create big trust.

Mindset Reps Journal Time

Where am I most tempted to cut corners, training, school, honesty, attitude, or friendships?

What is one small integrity choice I can make daily this week?

Is there any area where I act differently depending on who is watching? Why?

What does trust look like on a team, and how can I build it?

Ask God to strengthen your character. What do you want to be known for?

_____
_____
_____
_____
_____
_____
_____
_____
_____
_____

🙏 Prayer

God, help me be trustworthy in the small things.

Strengthen my integrity and my character.

Help me do what is right even when it is inconvenient.

Make me the same person in private and in public.

Teach me to honor You with my choices and to build trust with others.

Amen.

🔥 Weekly Challenge: Small Things

This week, choose one small integrity action and do it every day.

- finish warm-ups properly
- own mistakes quickly
- no gossip
- one minute with God
- extra reps done honestly

At the end of the week, write one sentence:

"This week, my integrity grew when..."

What you do when no one's watching is not invisible to God. It is the training ground for who you are becoming.

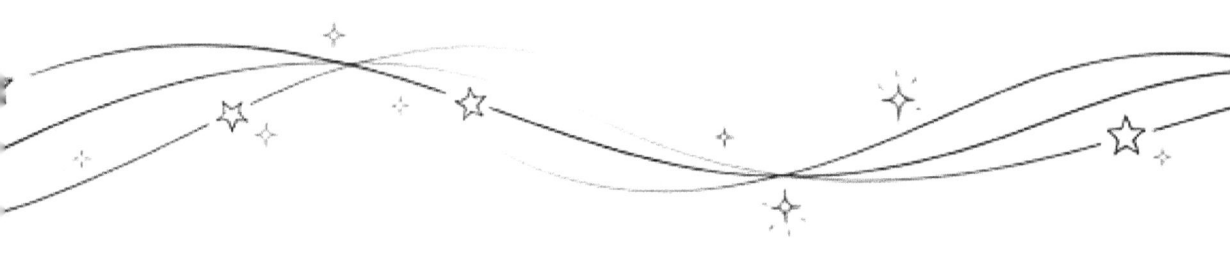

TWENTY-FIVE
Being Coachable

Coachability is humility in action.
It is how good athletes become great ones.

Whoever loves discipline loves knowledge, but whoever hates correction is stupid.

— **PROVERBS 12:1**

📖 When Correction Feels Personal

Honestly, being corrected can feel like being called out. Even when a coach is trying to help, your brain can interpret it as:

"I'm failing."
"I'm embarrassing."
"I'm not good enough."

Especially if correction happens in front of others, or if the coach's tone is blunt. Especially if you are already feeling insecure. But Proverbs 12:1 gives the truth without sugarcoating it: **loving discipline is wise**. That doesn't mean you have to enjoy correction, but you can choose to learn from it.

Coachability is one of the most important athlete skills, and it is not about being quiet or perfect. It's just about being teachable.

A coachable athlete:

- listens without rolling her eyes
- stays calm instead of arguing
- asks questions to understand
- applies feedback quickly
- does not take every correction as an insult

Here's the key:

Correction is about your actions, not your worth.

A coach correcting your positioning is not rejecting you as a person. A coach asking for more effort is not saying you are useless, and pushing you is often a sign that they believe you can grow.

This week, we are practicing humility. Not the "I'm small and worthless" kind, but the strong kind.

Humility says:

"I don't know everything yet, and that's okay."
"I can learn."
"I can improve."
"I can be corrected and still be confident."

Coachability is confidence that can handle feedback.

🎯 Game-Day Mindset: Correction Is Information

Try seeing feedback as data, not drama.

This Week's Cue Phrase:

☑ **"I'm here to learn."**

Say it when you feel defensive.

🏋 Training Room Application: The Coachable Response

Use this simple 3-step response when you get corrected.

1. Listen fully: Don't interrupt. Do not explain. Just listen.

2. Reply with one calm sentence

- "Got it."

- "Okay, I'll fix that."
- "Thanks, I'll adjust."
- "Can you show me the example?"

3. Apply it fast
The fastest way to rebuild confidence after correction is action. Do the next rep with the adjustment.

Extra tip: If the feedback is unclear, asking a question is not arguing, it's being coachable.

🧠 Mindset Reps Journal Time

🧠 What kind of correction makes me feel defensive, tone, public correction, or repeated feedback?

🧠 What story do I tell myself when I'm corrected?

🧠 What is a healthier truth I can choose instead?

🎯 What is one skill or habit I want to improve, and what feedback would help me?

🙏 Ask God to grow humility in you. Where do you need a softer heart and a stronger mindset?

_____
_____
_____
_____
_____
_____
_____
_____
_____
_____
_____

🙏 Prayer

God, help me be coachable.

When correction stings, help me stay calm and humble.

Teach me to learn quickly and respond with maturity.

Protect my heart from shame and pride.

Help me grow into the kind of person who loves truth and wants to improve.

Amen.

🔥 Weekly Challenge: Fast Adjustments

This week, choose one practice where you will focus on being extra coachable.

During that practice:

1. Listen fully to feedback.
2. Respond with: **"Got it."**
3. Apply the correction on the very next rep.

After practice, write one sentence:

"Today I was coachable when…"

Coachability doesn't imply that you can never mess up. It's about how quickly you learn, and that's a superpower.

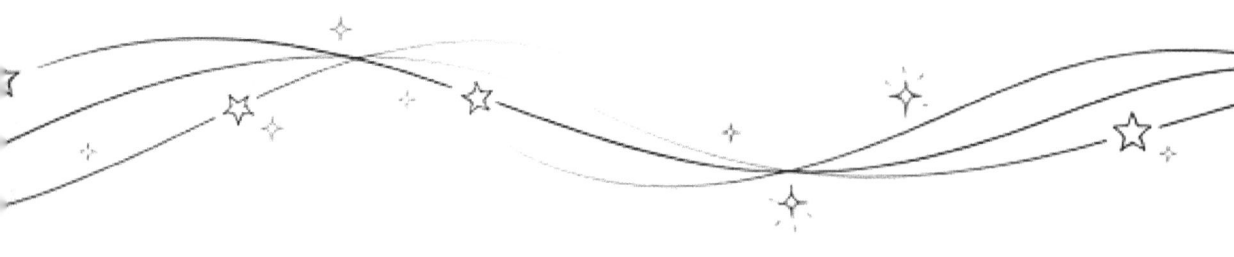

TWENTY-SIX
Excellence With Peace

You can aim high without living anxiously.

Do not be anxious about anything... And the peace of God... will guard your hearts and your minds in Christ Jesus.

— **PHILIPPIANS 4:6–7**

📖 High Standards, Low Panic

You can be a serious athlete and still be calm. You can want to improve and still have peace.

You can care deeply and still breathe.

But a lot of teen athletes feel like they have to choose one: Either you're intense and stressed, or you're chill and not trying. That's simply unnecessary. There's a difference between excellence and perfectionism.

Perfectionism says:

> "If it's not perfect, I'm not okay."

Excellence says:

> "I will give my best and keep learning."

Perfectionism makes us anxious, scared of mistakes, and it can also make you feel like you are never done. Philippians 4:6–7 is God's invitation to bring that anxious energy to Him. Not after you have everything sorted out. Right now.

God's peace doesn't mean you stop working hard, but that your hard work is not fueled by panic.

Excellence with peace looks like this:

- I prepare.
- I pray.
- I play hard.
- I release the outcome.

Peace guards your heart and mind. That means peace is protection, as it keeps your sport from taking over your identity. It keeps your thoughts from spiraling, and keeps you steady when pressure rises.

This week, your goal is to keep your **standards high** and your **nervous system calm**, because the best athletes are the steadiest.

🎯 Game-Day Mindset: Prepare, Then Release

You do your part. Then you hand the rest to God.

This Week's Cue Phrase:

✅ **"Excellence, not anxiety."**

Say it when you feel perfectionism creeping in.

🏋️ Training Room Application: The Peaceful Excellence Plan

Use this simple 3-part plan before practice, games, or tests.

1. Pick one excellence target, your focus for the day:

- effort
- communication
- calm under pressure
- finishing strong
- quick resets after mistakes

2. Breathe for 30 seconds

Slow inhale, longer exhale. Shoulders down.

3. Pray and release

> "God, I'll do my part. Please give me peace and help me trust You with the outcome."

This will keep your mind focused and your heart calm.

🧠 Mindset Reps Journal Time

🎯 What is the difference between excellence and perfectionism for me? How do I know when I've crossed the line?

😰 Where does anxiety show up most in my sport or school life?

🧠 What is one thought that triggers pressure, and what is a calmer, truer replacement thought?

What helps my body feel calm, breathing, music, prayer, stretching, talking to someone?

🙏 Write a short prayer you can use when you feel anxious before a game.

_____
_____
_____
_____
_____
_____
_____
_____
_____
_____
_____

🙏 Prayer

God, I want to pursue excellence without anxiety.

Help me work hard with a steady heart.

When pressure rises, teach me to bring my worries to You.

Guard my heart and mind with Your peace.

Help me play free, focused, and confident in You.

Amen.

🔥 Weekly Challenge: Peace Check

This week, before each practice or game:

1. Choose one excellence target.
2. Take 3 slow breaths.
3. Pray: "God, guard my mind with peace."

Afterward, write one sentence:

"Today I pursued excellence with peace when..."

Excellence is powerful. Peace is powerful. And together, they make you unshakeable.

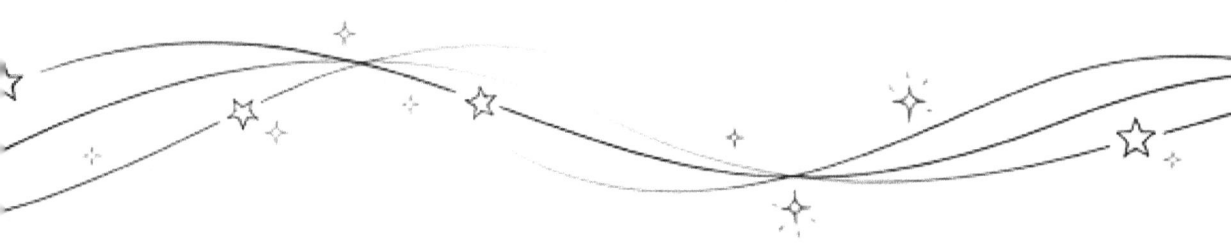

TWENTY-SEVEN
Calm Under Pressure

Pressure does not have to control you.

Calm is a skill you can practice.

You will keep in perfect peace those whose minds are steadfast, because they trust in You.

— **ISAIAH 26:3**

📖 Pressure Makes Everything Feel Louder

Pressure has a way of turning normal moments into huge moments.

Your heartbeat feels louder.
Your thoughts get faster.
Your hands feel sweaty.

Your brain starts shouting, "Don't mess up!"

Sometimes, the pressure isn't even from the game, but from what the game represents.

- I need to prove I belong.
- Everyone's watching.
- If I fail, I'll disappoint them.
- If I make a mistake, I'll be embarrassed.

Isaiah 26:3 gives a simple picture: peace comes from a steadfast mind that trusts God. A steadfast mind isn't a mind that never feels nervous. It's a mind that knows where to return. Calm isn't something you either have or don't have. **Calm is something you practice.**

Just like you practice footwork, passing, or shooting, you can practice calming your mind and body. God's peace is not just a vibe, it's a guard. It **protects your heart and mind** when pressure rises.

This week, we are practicing calm under pressure. Not by pretending you are not nervous, but by learning how to steady yourself and trust God in the moment. You can feel pressure and still play free.

🎯 GAME-DAY MINDSET: STEADY MIND, STEADY BODY

When your mind races, your body tightens. When your body tightens, your performance suffers. So calm the body first, and the mind will follow.

THIS WEEK'S CUE PHRASE:

✅ "Steady and ready."

🏋️ TRAINING ROOM APPLICATION: THE PRESSURE BREATHING DRILL

Use this during warm-up, timeouts, or between plays.

1. Inhale for 4 seconds
2. Exhale for 6 seconds
3. Repeat 3 times.

While you exhale, say in your mind:

"Steady and ready."

Then choose one focus point:

- Next play.
- Strong first touch.
- Communicate.
- Fast feet.

Longer exhales tell your nervous system that you are safe. Your brain can focus again.

🫘 Mindset Reps Journal Time

😬 What pressure moment affects me most, starting a game, taking a shot, serving, being watched, or making mistakes?

🧠 What thoughts show up when I feel pressure? Write them honestly.

 Which calm tool works best for me, breathing, prayer, cue phrase, or focusing on one job?

🎯 What is one simple focus point I can use when pressure rises?

🙏 How can I practice trusting God in the moment, not just before or after?

_____
_____
_____
_____
_____
_____
_____
_____
_____
_____

🙏 Prayer

God, when pressure rises, keep my mind steady.

Help me trust You and return to peace.

Teach me calm under pressure and focus in the moment.

Guard my heart and mind and help me play free.

Amen.

🔥 Weekly Challenge: Calm Reps

This week, practice your calm tool on purpose.

1. Do the 4-in, 6-out breathing for 3 rounds before practice.
2. Use your cue phrase during one pressure moment.
3. After practice or a game, write one sentence:

"Today, I stayed calm when..."

You're not trying to erase nerves, but training your nervous system to stay steady anyway.

TWENTY-EIGHT
When Anxiety Shows Up

Anxiety is loud, but it is not in charge.

You can carry it to God and keep moving.

Cast all your anxiety on Him because He cares for you.

— **1 PETER 5:7**

📖 THE SWIRL IN YOUR CHEST

Anxiety can show up in ways that do not always look dramatic, but feel very real. A tight chest, a shaky stomach, racing thoughts, overthinking every little thing, and feeling like something bad is about to happen, even when you can't explain why.

Sometimes anxiety shows up before games. Sometimes it shows up at school. Sometimes it shows up at night when you're trying to sleep and your brain decides it is time to panic about everything at once.

But anxiety doesn't mean you're weak. It means your mind and body are signaling stress. 1 Peter 5:7 says you can cast your anxiety on God because He cares for you. Notice what that verse doesn't say.

It doesn't say, "Fix yourself first, then come to God."

It doesn't say, "Stop feeling anxious or you are failing."

It says: *bring it*.

Casting anxiety is like taking something heavy out of your backpack and handing it to someone strong enough to carry it. You might still feel nervous after you pray, and that's normal, because prayer is not a magic switch. Prayer is a relationship, it's you saying, "God, I cannot carry this alone."

And when anxiety does show up, you can learn to respond with skill:

- breathe
- name what is happening
- tell God the truth
- do the next right thing

This week, your goal is not to never feel anxious. Your goal is to **handle anxiety in a healthier way**.

You are not alone. God cares, and He is close.

◎ GAME-DAY MINDSET: NAME IT, THEN MOVE

Anxiety grows when you pretend it is not there. It shrinks when you name it and take one small action.

THIS WEEK'S CUE PHRASE:

☑ **"I can carry this to God."**

🏋 TRAINING ROOM APPLICATION: THE 3-STEP ANXIETY RESET

Use this whenever anxiety shows up, before games, during school, or at night.

1. **Name it** - Say to yourself: "This is anxiety. Not danger."
2. **Breathe** - Inhale for 4 seconds, exhale for 6 seconds. Repeat 3 times.
3. **Cast it** - Pray one honest sentence: "God, I'm anxious about _____. Please help me. I give this to You."

Then do one small next step:

- drink water
- stretch
- talk to a trusted adult
- write it down
- start warm-up
- focus on one task

Small steps break the spiral.

📝 Mindset Reps Journal Time

😟 When does anxiety show up most for me, before games, at school, at night, or in social situations?

🎈 Where do I feel anxiety in my body, tight chest, stomach, headaches, restlessness?

💭 What is one thought that fuels my anxiety, and what truth can replace it?

👤 Who is one safe person I can talk to if anxiety feels too big?

🙏 Write a one-sentence prayer based on 1 Peter 5:7 that you can use anytime.

_____
_____
_____
_____
_____
_____
_____
_____
_____
_____
_____
_____

🙏 Prayer

God, You care about me.

When anxiety shows up, help me not panic or hide.

Teach me to bring it to You honestly.

Give me calm, courage, and the next right step.

Help me trust that I am not alone.

Amen.

🔥 Weekly Challenge: Cast It

This week, every time anxiety shows up:

1. Name it: "This is anxiety."
2. Breathe: 4 in, 6 out, three times.
3. Cast it: one honest sentence to God.
4. Do the next right thing.

At the end of the week, write one sentence:

"When I cast my anxiety to God, I noticed…"

Anxiety may be loud, but God's care is louder, and it will keep you steady.

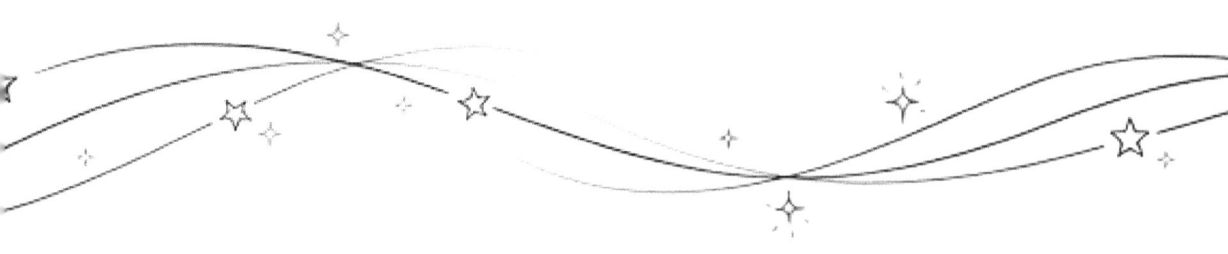

TWENTY-NINE
The Fear of Failure Trap

Failure is something that happens, not something you are.

Trust in the Lord with all your heart... and He will make your paths straight.

— **PROVERBS 3:5–6**

📖 When Fear Makes You Play Safe

Fear of failure doesn't always look like panic. Sometimes it looks like playing small. Sometimes you stop taking risks. You stop trying new skills. You pass the ball fast so you cannot be blamed. You hesitate. You hold back. You choose "safe" over "brave."

Because deep down, you're thinking:

"If I fail, I'll prove I'm not good."
"If I fail, people will judge me."
"If I fail, I'll be embarrassed."
"If I fail, I'll disappoint everyone."

Unfortunately, fear of failure makes you avoid the very things that help you grow, and it can turn sport into a test where you're constantly trying not to mess up.

Proverbs 3:5–6 calls you to trust God, not your ability to control outcomes. Trusting God means you can try hard without needing a guarantee, you can take a risk without knowing exactly how it will go, and you can fail and still be okay.

God does not love you less when you struggle. He is not embarrassed by your learning process. Failure can feel scary, but it is also part of growth. It teaches you, stretches you, and it builds resilience.

> When you stop treating failure like a disaster, **you become freer**.

So this week, the goal is not to avoid failure. The goal is to stop fearing it so much that it controls you.

🎯 Game-Day Mindset: Brave Over Perfect

You do not need perfect. You need progress.

This Week's Cue Phrase:

☑ **"I can try and trust."**

Try your best. Trust God with the rest.

🏋️ Training Room Application: The Risk Reps Plan

This week, choose one area where you tend to play safe. Then, commit to taking small risks on purpose.

Pick one:

- Attempt the new move 5 times this week
- Push pace during conditioning instead of holding back
- Communicate loudly even if you feel shy
- Take the open shot instead of passing out of fear
- Ask your coach for feedback on one weak skill

When you take a risk, remind yourself:

> Trying is not failing. **Trying is training**.

Mindset Reps Journal Time

What kind of failure scares me most, mistakes in games, looking silly, letting people down, or not being "good enough"?

When I fear failure, how does it change the way I play?

What is one risk rep I can take this week that would help me grow?

Write about a time I failed but learned something valuable. What did it teach me?

What does trusting God look like when I do not know how things will turn out?

_____
_____
_____
_____
_____
_____
_____
_____
_____
_____

🙏 Prayer

God, help me trust You more than I trust my need to control outcomes.

Free me from fear of failure.

Give me courage to try, learn, and grow.

When I mess up, help me reset and keep going.

Lead me on a straight path and steady my heart.

Amen.

🔥 Weekly Challenge: Try Anyway

This week, do one thing you have been avoiding because you might fail.

1. Say: **"I can try and trust."**
2. Take the risk rep.
3. Afterward, write one sentence:

"I grew today because I…"

Fear wants you to play small, while faith helps you play free. And from this point onward, you are choosing freedom.

THIRTY
Playing Free

Freedom helps you play your best.
Tightness steals your game.

Where the Spirit of the Lord is, there is freedom.

— **2 CORINTHIANS 3:17**

📖 When Your Body Feels Like It Forgot How to Sport

You know that horrible feeling when you're in your head and everything feels awkward? Your legs feel heavy, your timing feels off, and your decisions feel slow. You overthink every move and start trying to control everything.

That's playing tight.

Playing tight is what happens when fear, pressure, or perfectionism takes over your body. It's like your mind grabs the steering wheel and your instincts panic. The crazy part is that you can be fully trained and still play tight. Because tightness is not about skill, but about freedom.

2 Corinthians 3:17 says where the Spirit of the Lord is, there is freedom. God is not trying to make you anxious. He is not trying to crush you with pressure.

He invites you into freedom.

Freedom doesn't mean you don't care. Freedom means you're not controlled by fear.

Freedom says:

- I can make mistakes and still be okay.
- I can play hard without trying to be perfect.
- I can focus on the moment, not the outcome.
- I can trust God with what I cannot control.

When you play free, your body moves better, your instincts work, and your confidence feels calmer. You are present. So, this week is about letting go of tightness and practicing freedom.

🎯 Game-Day Mindset: Loose Body, Clear Mind

A calm body supports a calm mind.

This Week's Cue Phrase:
✅ **"Play free."**

🛡️ Training Room Application: The "Loose and Ready" Routine

Use this before games or any time you notice tightness.

1. **Three slow breaths**: Inhale for 4, exhale for 6.

2. **Loosen your body**: Shake out hands, roll shoulders, unclench jaw.

3. **Choose one simple job.** Pick a focus:

   - communicate
   - hustle back
   - strong first touch
   - quick feet
   - stay positive

4. **One-line prayer**

> "God, help me play free and trust You."

This routine will help your body stop bracing for failure.

🪨 Mindset Reps Journal Time

😊 When do I play tight most often, at the start, after mistakes, when being watched, or in close games?

🧠 What thoughts make me tense, and what truth could replace them?

✋ What does playing free look like for me in my sport? Be specific.

🎯 What is one simple job I can focus on when I feel tight?

🙏 What would it look like to invite God into the pressure moment instead of trying to handle it alone?

_____
_____
_____
_____
_____
_____
_____
_____
_____
_____
_____
_____

🙏 Prayer

God, I want to play with freedom, not fear.

When pressure makes me tense, help me breathe and release control.

Fill me with Your peace and help me trust You in the moment.

Teach me to focus on the next play and enjoy the game again.

Amen.

🔥 Weekly Challenge: Freedom Moment

This week, choose one moment in a game or practice where you usually get tight.

When it happens:

1. Take one slow breath.
2. Say: **"Play free."**
3. Do your one simple job.

Afterward, write one sentence:

"I played freer when I…"

Tightness is a habit, but so is freedom. You are training the better one.

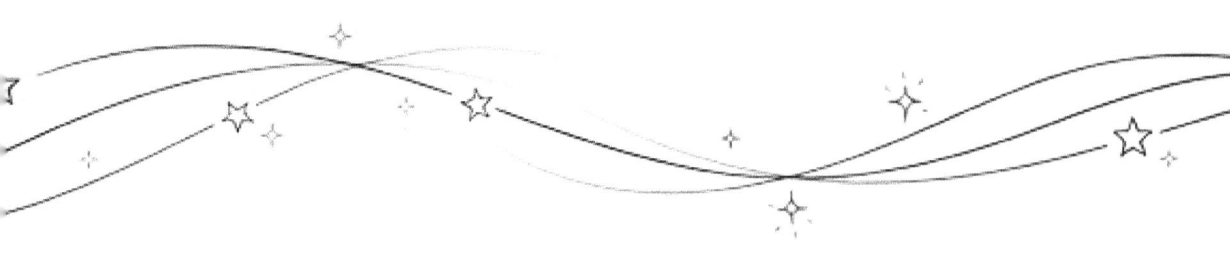

THIRTY-ONE
Confidence After a Bad Game

A bad game is feedback, not a forecast.

The Lord is close to the brokenhearted and saves those who are crushed in spirit.

— **PSALM 34:18**

📖 The Car Ride Home

Bad games hit different. Sometimes you know you played poorly. Sometimes you tried your hardest and it still did not go well, or one mistake feels like it ruined everything. Sometimes you're not even sure what happened, you just felt off.

And then comes the worst part for a lot of athletes: the after. The replaying and the embarrassment. The "everyone thinks I'm terrible" thoughts. The urge to quit. The car ride home where you either get a lecture or you sit in silence and your brain does the lecturing for everyone.

Psalm 34:18 says God is close to the brokenhearted. That includes sports heartbreak. God is not rolling His eyes at you because it is "just a game." He cares because you care.

So what do you do after a bad game?

You don't pretend it didn't happen. You don't punish yourself for days. You don't decide you are worthless.

> You do what strong athletes do:
> You recover well.

Confidence isn't pretending you're always good, but believing you can **learn, reset, and come back**. A bad game is just a moment, not your identity.

It's valuable feedback, and God's closeness means **you do not have to carry shame alone**. This week is about rebuilding confidence the right way. Not with denial, but with wisdom, kindness, and a plan.

🎯 Game-Day Mindset: Review, Then Release

Strong athletes do a short review and then they let it go.

This Week's Cue Phrase:

✅ **"Learn it, then leave it."**

🏥 Training Room Application: The 24-Hour Reset Plan

Use this after a bad game or a rough practice.

1. **Cool down your emotions**

Eat something, drink water, shower, sleep. Don't do a full life review at 11 pm.

2. **Do a 5-minute review only** - answer three questions:

   - What went well?
   - What did not go well?
   - What is one thing I will work on next?

3. **Make a micro-plan** - Choose one small action for the next practice:

   - focus on first touch
   - stay wide
   - breathe before free throws
   - communicate early
   - hustle back on defense

4. **Give it to God**

> "God, I'm disappointed. Help me learn and move forward."

🌀 Mindset Reps Journal Time

😔 What do I usually do after a bad game, shut down, spiral, overtrain, or avoid everyone?

💭 What is the harshest thought I tell myself after I play poorly?

✏️ What would it sound like to speak to myself with the same kindness I would give a teammate? Write one sentence.

🎯 If I could redo one moment from the game, what would I do differently? What skill does that point to?

🙏 What do I need to tell God honestly about how I feel right now?

_____
_____
_____
_____
_____
_____
_____
_____
_____
_____

🙏 Prayer

God, I feel disappointed and frustrated.

Thank You for being close to me when my heart feels heavy.

Help me learn from what happened without drowning in shame.

Give me courage to try again and wisdom to grow.

Remind me that my worth does not change with my performance.

Amen.

🔥 Weekly Challenge: 10-Minute Review

The next time you have a rough game or practice:

1. Set a timer for 10 minutes.
2. Write: 1 win, 1 lesson, 1 next step.
3. Pray one honest sentence.
4. When the timer ends, stop replaying.

Afterward, write one sentence:

"I rebuilt my confidence by…"

You are not defined by your worst day. You are defined by how you respond and how you rise.

THIRTY-TWO
Bounce Back Faster

Falling is part of growth.

Staying down is optional.

Though I have fallen, I will rise.

— **MICAH 7:8**

📖 The Difference Between Falling and Staying Down

Every athlete falls in some way. Sometimes it's a literal fall, other times it's a mistake. Sometimes it's a bad season, a confidence crash, or getting cut, benched, injured, or overlooked.

However, falling is not the problem. In fact, falling is normal. Staying down is the problem. Micah 7:8 is such a powerful sentence:

> **"Though I have fallen, I will rise."**

Not "I might rise if I feel like it."

Not "I will rise if nobody saw me fall."

I will rise. That's **resilience**.

Now, resilience isn't pretending things don't hurt. It's feeling it, then choosing to get up anyway. And here is the secret: bouncing back faster is a skill you can practice. Some athletes lose one moment and stay stuck in it for the rest of the game, while others recover quickly. They reset, they move on, and they **stay present and focused**. This week, God is helping you build that kind of strength.

You will have moments when you fall, but you don't have to live there.

🎯 Game-Day Mindset: Fall, Reset, Rise

You do not need a dramatic comeback story in one second. You just need the next right step.

This week's cue phrase:

✅ **"I rise."**

Say it after mistakes. Say it after setbacks. Say it when you feel like hiding.

🏋 Training Room Application: The Bounce-Back Routine

Use this routine when something goes wrong.

✓ Name it quickly

- "That was a mistake."
- "That hurt."
- "That was disappointing."

✓ Breathe once. Slow exhale. Drop your shoulders.

✓ Choose your reset phrase

- "I rise."
- "Next play."
- "I can adjust"

✓ Do one action that moves you forward

- get back on defense
- ask your coach what to fix
- take the next shot
- redo the drill
- encourage a teammate
- start your rehab rep

🪨 Mindset Reps Journal Time

🪨 What kind of setbacks hit me hardest, mistakes, criticism, injuries, or being overlooked?

⏳ How long do I usually stay stuck after something goes wrong?

💭 What is my go-to reset phrase for this week? Write it clearly.

🎯 What is one "forward action" I can take when I feel disappointed?

🙏 Where do I need God's help to rise again right now?

_____
_____
_____
_____
_____
_____
_____
_____
_____
_____
_____
_____

🙏 Prayer

God, when I fall, help me rise.

Give me resilience and courage to keep going.

Teach me to reset quickly and not live in shame.

When I feel discouraged, remind me that You are with me.

Help me move forward with faith and strength.

Amen.

🔥 Weekly Challenge: I Rise

This week, when you mess up or feel discouraged:

1. Take one slow breath.
2. Say: **"I rise."**
3. Do one forward action immediately.

After practice or the game, write one sentence:

"Today, I rose when..."

You're not building a life where you never fall. You're building a life where you always get back up.

THIRTY-THREE
Control the Controllables

Peace comes from focusing on what you can control and releasing what you cannot.

Let your yes be yes and your no be no.

— **MATTHEW 5:37**

📖 When Everything Feels Out of Your Hands

Some parts of sport feel unfair. You can train hard and still not start, or play well and still lose. You can get better and still get criticized. You can even do everything right and still deal with bad calls, bad timing, or bad luck. And when things feel out of your control, it is easy to spiral into frustration:

- "What's the point?"
- "It's not fair."
- "I can't win."
- "Why do I even try?"

Matthew 5:37 is Jesus telling you to be simple and steady. Let your yes be yes, and your no be no. In other words: do not get pulled into chaos.

Stay clear. Stay grounded.

A huge part of mental toughness is learning what belongs to you and what does not.

What belongs to you:

- your effort
- your attitude
- your preparation
- your focus
- your choices
- your response after mistakes

What does not belong to you:

- the referee
- the coach's decisions
- other people's moods

- the weather
- the crowd
- the final outcome every time

When you focus on what you can't control, you feel powerless. However, when you focus on what you can control, you feel steady. You become the kind of athlete who stays calm and consistent no matter what the conditions are. God is teaching you to live with clarity.

Do your part, then trust Him with the rest.

🎯 Game-Day Mindset: My Circle, Not the Chaos

Imagine a circle around you. Inside it are your controllables. Outside it is noise.

This Week's Cue Phrase:

☑ **"Back to my circle."**

Say it when you feel distracted by drama, unfairness, or frustration.

🏋️ Training Room Application: The Circle List

Before a game or practice, write two quick lists.

1. **Inside my circle (I control):**

   - hustle
   - communication
   - calm breathing
   - quick reset after mistakes

2. **Outside my circle (I release):**

- ref calls
- who starts
- other people's opinions

Then pray one sentence:

> "God, help me focus on my circle and release the rest."

This is a powerful way to calm your mind fast.

Mindset Reps Journal Time

- What do I waste the most energy worrying about that I cannot control?

- How does focusing on the uncontrollables affect my performance and mood?

- List 3 controllables I want to focus on this week. Make them specific.

- List 2 things I need to release to God because they are outside my circle.

- What does it look like for me to trust God with the outcome while still giving full effort?

_____
_____
_____
_____
_____
_____
_____
_____
_____
_____
_____
_____

🙏 Prayer

God, help me focus on what I can control.

When I feel frustrated by unfairness or things outside my hands, bring me back to peace.

Teach me clarity and steadiness.

Help me do my part with excellence and trust You with the rest.

Amen.

🔥 Weekly Challenge: Back to My Circle

This week, when something frustrating happens that you cannot control:

1. Take one slow breath.
2. Say: **"Back to my circle."**
3. Choose one controllable action immediately: hustle, communicate, reset, encourage.

After practice or a game, write one sentence:

"Today, I stayed steady by focusing on…"

You can't control everything, but you can control your response. And that's where your power is.

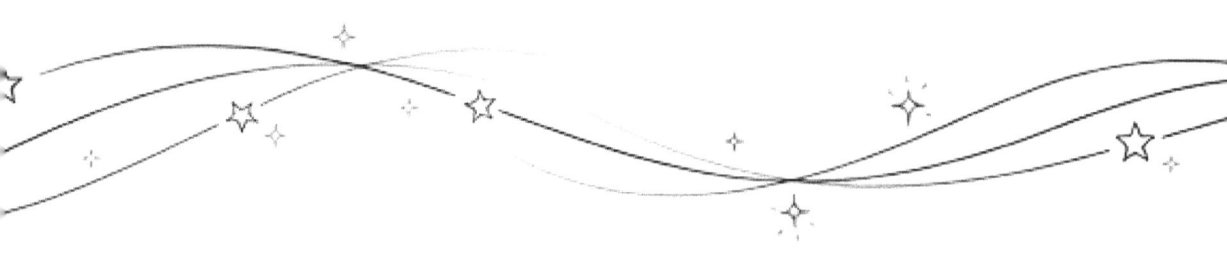

THIRTY-FOUR
Strength With Kindness

Being tough does not mean being harsh.

Real strength includes gentleness.

Be strong and courageous... Do not be afraid... for the Lord your God goes with you.

— **DEUTERONOMY 31:6**

📖 Tough Girl Does Not Have to Mean Hard Girl

A lot of athletes think toughness has one look.

No tears.
No softness.
No sensitivity.
No asking for help.
No showing you care too much.

Basically, you're supposed to be a human brick wall. But that version of toughness can turn you into someone you do not even like.

Harshness is not the same as strength. Real strength is being able to feel things and still stay steady. Real strength is being competitive without being cruel, and being confident without needing to put someone else down.

Deuteronomy 31:6 says be strong and courageous because God goes with you. Notice it does not say, "Be strong and mean." God's strength does not make you cold; it makes you grounded.

Strength with kindness looks like:

- you push yourself, but you do not bully yourself
- you hold teammates accountable, but you do it with respect
- you compete hard, but you keep your character clean
- you are brave enough to be kind when others are being petty

Kindness is not weakness. It takes courage to stay kind when you are stressed, tired, or annoyed. So, this week, you are practicing a powerful combination: strong and kind.

You can be a **fierce athlete** and still have a **soft heart**.

🎯 Game-Day Mindset: Fierce and Respectful

You do not have to choose between being intense and being kind.

This week's cue phrase:
☑ **"Strong and kind."**

Say it when you feel tempted to snap, roll your eyes, or shut down.

🏋️ Training Room Application: The Kindness Strength Plan

Pick one way to practice strength with kindness this week.

- **Encourage someone** who is struggling, even if you are focused on your own performance
- **Speak respectfully** when giving feedback to a teammate
- **Self-kindness** after mistakes, use supportive self-talk instead of harsh words
- **Ask for help** when you need it instead of pretending you are fine
- **Stay calm** when drama tries to pull you in

This is true leadership.

🍃 Mindset Reps Journal Time

💬 When do I become harsh, toward myself or others? What usually triggers it?

🍃 What does "strong and kind" look like for me in my sport, specifically?

Write one sentence of self-talk I can use after mistakes that is firm but kind.

🍃 How do I want to be remembered by my teammates, for my talent, my attitude, or both?

🙏 Ask God to help you be strong and kind. What area do you need His help with most?

_____
_____
_____
_____
_____
_____
_____
_____
_____
_____

🙏 Prayer

God, make me strong and courageous, and keep my heart kind.

Help me compete with intensity and integrity.

Teach me to speak with respect, even when I am stressed.

Help me treat myself with kindness while still pursuing growth.

Give me Your strength that does not harden my heart.

Amen.

🔥 Weekly Challenge: One Kind Choice

This week, make one kind choice every day, especially when you feel stressed.

- encourage a teammate
- speak gently instead of snapping
- replace harsh self-talk with truth
- ask for help
- choose calm over drama

At the end of the week, write one sentence:

"This week, I was strong and kind when…"

Strong and kind isn't soft. It's powerful, and it's exactly the kind of strength that lasts.

THIRTY-FIVE
Team First, Ego Last

The best teammates make the whole team better, even when they are not the star.

Do nothing out of selfish ambition or vain conceit. Rather, in humility value others above yourselves.

— **PHILIPPIANS 2:3**

📖 Being a Great Teammate Is a Skill

It's easy to say "teamwork" and post a cute quote about it.

However, it's harder to live it when:

- you want more minutes
- you do not like someone's attitude
- you feel overlooked
- someone else is getting the praise
- the coach is choosing favourites
- the team group chat is too much

Team sports can bring out the best in people. They can also bring out jealousy, insecurity, and ego. Philippians 2:3 talks about humility and valuing others. That doesn't mean you become a doormat. It means you stop making everything about you.

A team-first athlete:

- celebrates others without shrinking herself
- encourages even when she is frustrated
- stays positive when things are messy
- works hard even when she is not in the spotlight
- owns mistakes without blaming

Your character is part of your contribution. Even if you're not the top scorer, you can still change the whole environment. Teams don't fall apart because of lack of talent; they fall apart because of ego, negativity, and drama.

This week, God is calling you to train **humility** and **leadership**.

Ego says, "What about me?"

Humility says, "How can I help the team?"

A humble mindset makes you a stronger athlete and a stronger person.

🎯 Game-Day Mindset: Add Value

Instead of asking, "Am I getting enough attention?" ask, "Am I adding value?"

This week's cue phrase:

☑ **"I build my team."**

Say it when you feel jealousy or irritation rising.

🏋️ Training Room Application: The Teammate Upgrade

Pick one teammate habit to practice this week.

- **Encourage** one teammate every practice with something specific
- **Communicate** more even if you feel shy
- **Stay calm** in tense moments and help reset the mood
- **Celebrate** someone else when they do well
- **Do the unglamorous work** like defense, hustle, clean passes, setting screens
- **Own your mistakes** fast and move on

Team-first choices are not loud, but they are powerful.

Mindset Reps Journal Time

What team situation triggers my ego the most, minutes, praise, roles, or comparisons?

What does humility look like for me without shrinking myself?

How can I add value to my team this week, even if I am not the star?

Who on my team do I need to celebrate more, and why?

Ask God to help you value others and build a healthy team spirit. What do you need help with?

_____
_____
_____
_____
_____
_____
_____
_____
_____
_____
_____

🙏 Prayer

God, help me be a teammate who builds, not breaks.

Grow humility in me and free me from jealousy and ego.

Teach me to value others and to bring positive energy to my team.

Help me work hard, encourage others, and play with integrity.

Make me the kind of athlete who makes the whole team stronger.

Amen.

🔥 Weekly Challenge: Build the Team

This week, do one team-building action at every practice or game:

- encourage someone
- celebrate someone else
- reset the mood when it gets tense
- do the unglamorous work
- communicate clearly

After practice, write one sentence:

"Today, I built my team when…"

Being a team-first athlete is not about losing your shine. It's about becoming the kind of leader who helps everyone shine.

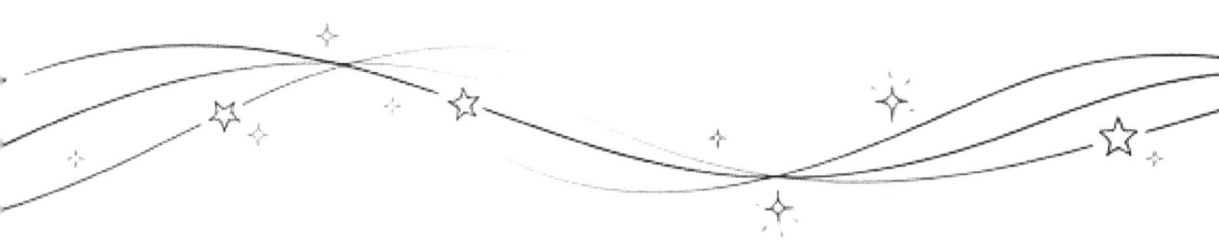

THIRTY-SIX

Handling Jealousy and Comparison

You can admire someone else's success without hating yourself.

A heart at peace gives life to the body, but envy rots the bones.

— **PROVERBS 14:30**

📖 WHEN SOMEONE ELSE GETS WHAT YOU WANTED

Jealousy is one of those emotions nobody wants to admit, but almost everyone feels. It hits when:

- someone else gets the starting spot
- your teammate gets praised and you get ignored
- a friend makes a rep team
- someone posts highlights and everyone freaks out
- your crush cheers for another girl
- your coach seems to trust someone else more

And then your brain goes into comparison mode:

> "She's better than me."
> "I'll never catch up."
> "Why do I even try?"
> "Of course they like her."
> "Maybe I'm not meant for this."

Proverbs 14:30 says envy rots the bones. That sounds intense, but it's actually accurate. Envy doesn't just hurt emotionally. It drains you, steals your peace, makes you bitter, and it can even make you act like someone you don't recognize.

Jealousy usually points to something you care about deeply. It might point to a goal you want, a fear you have, or a place where you need healing. God does not shame you for feeling jealousy, but invites you to handle it wisely.

You can do three things with jealousy:

1. deny it and let it grow in secret
2. feed it and let it turn into bitterness
3. **face it and let it become fuel for growth**

This week, we're choosing option 3. You can admire someone else's talent and still believe God has a place for you. Someone else's success does not cancel your future. You're not in a race against your teammates. You're in a **growth process with God.**

🎯 Game-Day Mindset: Bless, Then Build

A powerful way to break jealousy is to bless the person and then focus on your own work.

This week's cue phrase:

☑ **"I'm in my lane."**

🏋 Training Room Application: The Jealousy Reset

Use this when jealousy shows up.

Name it: "I feel jealous."

Bless: Say one of these quietly:

- "God, bless her."
- "I'm happy for her."
- "Her win is not my loss."

Build: Choose one action to help you grow:

- ask your coach what to work on
- do extra reps on a weak skill
- set a small goal for the week
- encourage someone instead of withdrawing

🖊 Mindset Reps Journal Time

😟 What situation triggers jealousy for me most often in sport or friendships?

💭 What story do I tell myself when someone else succeeds?

🛤 What does staying "in my lane" look like for me this week?

🎯 What is one goal I can focus on that is about my growth, not beating someone else?

🙏 Ask God for a heart at peace. What do you need help letting go of?

_____
_____
_____
_____
_____
_____
_____
_____
_____
_____

🙏 Prayer

God, I want a heart at peace.

When jealousy shows up, help me not feed it.

Teach me to celebrate others and still believe You have good plans for me.

Free me from comparison and bitterness.

Help me stay in my lane, focused, grateful, and growing.

Amen.

🔥 Weekly Challenge: Bless and Build

This week, when you feel jealousy:

1. Name it.
2. Bless the person with a short prayer.
3. Do one growth action within 24 hours.

Afterward, write one sentence:

"This week, I handled jealousy in a healthier way when..."

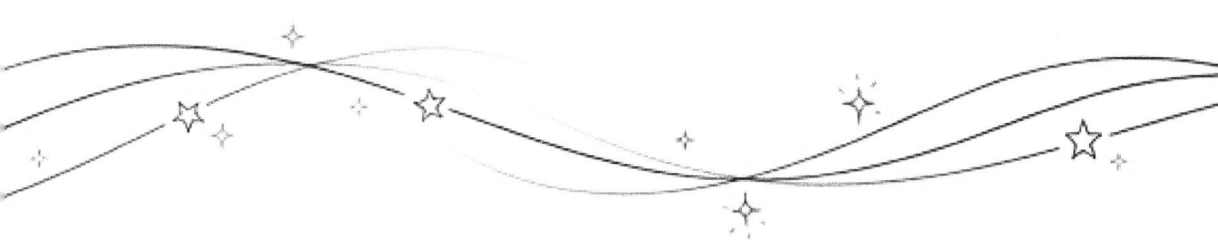

THIRTY-SEVEN
Lead Without Being Loud

You do not need to be the loudest person to be a leader.

Let no one despise you for your youth, but set the believers an example...

— **1 TIMOTHY 4:12**

📖 Leadership Is Not a Personality Type

A lot of girls think leadership looks like one thing:

> Confident. Loud. Outgoing. Always talking. Always in charge.

But real leadership is not about volume; it's about influence. You can be quiet and still lead. You can be shy and still set an example. You can be new to the team and still raise the standard.

1 Timothy 4:12 is powerful because it says your age does not cancel your ability to lead. Your youth does not make you irrelevant. God can use you right now.

Leadership is how you show up when things get hard.

It looks like:

- being consistent when others are moody
- staying respectful when others get sarcastic
- encouraging a teammate who is struggling
- working hard without needing attention
- apologizing quickly when you mess up
- choosing integrity over drama

The truth is, teams need different kinds of leaders. They need the hype leader who brings energy, the steady leader who brings calm, and the brave leader who speaks up. They also need the loyal leader who shows up and does the work.

If you're not naturally loud, that's not a problem. Your leadership can look like steadiness. This week, God is inviting you to lead by example. Not by trying to be someone else, but by being faithful, consistent, and courageous in your own way.

🎯 Game-Day Mindset: Example Over Attention

Leadership is not trying to be noticed, it is choosing to be consistent.

This week's cue phrase:

☑ **"I set the tone."**

Even if you say nothing, your attitude sets a tone.

💪 Training Room Application: The Quiet Leader Plan

Pick one way to lead this week. Keep it simple and real.

✔ **Encourage one teammate** each practice

✔ **Stay calm** when others get stressed

✔ **Communicate clearly** even if you are nervous

✔ **Go first** in effort, sprint back, hustle, warm-ups

✔ **Be coachable** and apply feedback fast

✔ **Do the unglamorous work** without complaining

🖊 Mindset Reps Journal Time

What kind of leader do I naturally want to be, calm, encouraging, brave, consistent, or energetic?

What is one leadership action that fits my personality?

🎯 Where does my team need a better tone, effort, kindness, focus, or unity?

🎤 Is there one moment I should speak up this week, even if it feels scary? What would I say?

🙏 Ask God to help you lead. What example do you want to set?

_____
_____
_____
_____
_____
_____
_____
_____
_____
_____

🙏 Prayer

God, help me lead in a way that honors You.

Give me courage to set a good example, even when I feel young or unsure.

Help me influence my team with consistency, kindness, and integrity.

Show me when to speak up and when to stay steady.

Use my life to set the tone for good.

Amen.

🔥 Weekly Challenge: Set the Tone

This week, choose one moment at each practice where you will lead by example.
Examples:

- arrive focused
- do warm-ups properly
- encourage someone
- respond calmly to mistakes
- keep your attitude steady

After practice, write one sentence:

"Today I set the tone when…"

You don't have to be loud to be powerful. Your example will speak volumes.

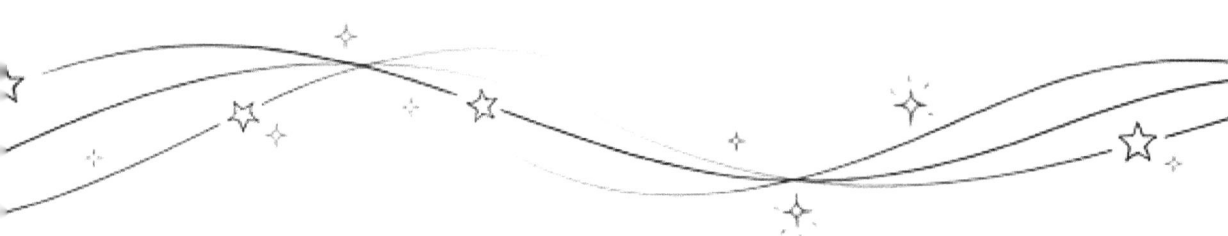

THIRTY-EIGHT
When You Feel Unseen

God sees you fully, even when people miss you.

Nothing in all creation is hidden from God's sight.

— **HEBREWS 4:13**

📖 THE QUIET ACHE OF BEING OVERLOOKED

There is a specific kind of sadness that comes from feeling unseen. You work hard, but nobody mentions it. You improve, but nobody notices. You show up early, stay late, do the extras, and still feel invisible.

Sometimes it's in sport. Sometimes it's at school. Sometimes it's in friendships, where you are the one who checks in, but nobody checks in on you. And when you feel unseen long enough, it can turn into thoughts like:

> "Why do I even try?"

> "No one cares."

> "Maybe I don't matter."

> "If I disappeared, would anyone notice?"

Hebrews 4:13 is a steady truth for moments like this: **nothing is hidden from God's sight**. That means your effort is not invisible, your tears are not invisible, your private battles are not invisible, and your growth is not invisible. God sees you in the parts nobody claps for.

Now, honestly, I know it still hurts when people don't notice, and you're allowed to feel that. But here's what you don't want to do: You don't want to let feeling unseen make you quit becoming who God is shaping you to be. Being unseen by people doesn't mean you're unimportant, it just means people are limited. God is not.

Sometimes, God grows you in hidden seasons. Not because you are being punished, but because you are being built. *Roots grow underground first.*

. . .

If you're in a season where you feel overlooked, this week is about anchoring your identity in the One who sees you.

🎯 GAME-DAY MINDSET: SEEN BY GOD, STEADY IN ME

When you feel invisible, you are tempted to do one of two things:

- try to get attention in unhealthy ways
- shrink and stop trying

Instead, choose steadiness.

THIS WEEK'S CUE PHRASE:

☑ **"God sees me."**

Say it when you feel overlooked.

🏋️ TRAINING ROOM APPLICATION: THE UNSEEN WORK PLAN

This week, choose one "unseen" action you will keep doing with excellence, even if nobody mentions it.

- Finish warm-ups properly
- Do the unglamorous defensive work
- Encourage teammates quietly
- Stay coachable and calm
- Sleep and recover well
- Spend one minute with God daily

Then remind yourself:

God sees the work. The work is shaping me.

Mindset Reps Journal Time

😌 Where do I feel the most unseen right now, sport, friendships, family, or school?

🕊️ What do I start believing about myself when I feel overlooked?

♡ Write a truth statement based on Hebrews 4:13 that you want to remember.

🎯 What is one unseen habit or effort I can keep doing with excellence this week?

🙏 Ask God to comfort you and remind you of your worth. What do you need to tell Him honestly?

_____
_____
_____
_____
_____
_____
_____
_____
_____
_____
_____

🙏 Prayer

God, You see me completely.

When I feel overlooked, remind me that I am not invisible to You.

Comfort my heart and help me stay steady.

Give me strength to keep doing what is right with excellence.

Help me trust that You are working in me even in hidden seasons.

Amen.

🔥 Weekly Challenge: Unseen Excellence

This week, do one unseen act of excellence every day, for example:

- finish a drill strong
- do the extra stretch
- speak kindly when nobody's watching
- encourage someone quietly
- pray for one minute

At the end of the week, write one sentence:

"Even when I felt unseen, I stayed steady by…"

People may miss you sometimes, but God does not, and His view, along with yours, are the ones that matter most.

THIRTY-NINE

Letting Go of Approval

You can respect people's opinions without living for them.

Am I now trying to win the approval of human beings, or of God? ... If I were still trying to please people, I would not be a servant of Christ.

— **GALATIANS 1:10**

📖 When You Feel Like Everyone's Watching

Approval is sneaky. It can look like being motivated, but underneath it is fear. Perhaps it's fear of disappointing your coach, and fear of being judged by teammates. Or, fear of what people think in the stands, fear of looking silly, and fear of being talked about.

As a teen girl, approval pressure can feel extra intense because you're juggling sport and social life at the same time.

You're trying to be:

- talented
- likeable
- confident
- not too confident
- chill but not lazy
- kind but not "soft"

Girl. That's *so* exhausting.

Galatians 1:10 asks a sharp question: whose approval are you chasing? Because if your confidence depends on other people's opinions, you'll never feel steady. Opinions change, and people are inconsistent. One day you're the hero, the next day you're "mid."

God's approval is different. It's not earned by being perfect, but simply given. That doesn't mean you stop caring about growth or feedback, but you can stop needing people to like you in order to feel okay.

When you play for approval, you play tight. **When you play from identity, you play free.**

This week, you're going to practice a powerful shift: I can be kind and respectful, but I don't need to be liked by everyone.

🌀 Game-Day Mindset: Identity First

Your performance is something you do. It is not who you are.

This Week's Cue Phrase:

☑ **"God's opinion is my anchor."**

Use it when you feel the pressure to impress.

🏋 Training Room Application: The Approval Detox

This week, practice one of these:

1. **Before practice, set an internal goal**: Choose a goal that has nothing to do with praise: effort, communication, calm, discipline.

2. **Do one brave thing without seeking validation**: Take the shot. Ask the question. Speak up. Try the new skill. No fishing for compliments.

3. **Limit social media after games**: If you tend to check likes, views, or comments for emotional proof, give yourself a break.

4. **Hand the pressure to God**: Pray: "God, I want to honor You more than I want approval."

The goal isn't to stop caring, but to stop needing applause to feel secure.

Mindset Reps Journal Time

- Whose approval do I care about most, and why?

- How does approval pressure affect my performance or mood?

- Write a truth statement that anchors me in God's approval, not people's opinions.

- What internal goal can I focus on this week that is fully in my control?

- What pressure do I need to give to God today?

_____
_____
_____
_____
_____
_____
_____
_____
_____
_____
_____
_____

🙏 Prayer

God, free me from living for other people's approval.

Help me care about growth without being controlled by opinions.

Anchor my confidence in You.

Teach me to play with freedom and integrity, and to trust that You are pleased when I live with faith and courage.

Amen.

🔥 Weekly Challenge: Internal Win

This week, after every practice or game, write one internal win:

"Today, I'm proud of myself because I..."

Examples:

- stayed calm under pressure
- encouraged a teammate
- took a risk
- reset quickly
- gave full effort

Your worth is not a popularity contest. God's approval is steady, and you can build your life on that.

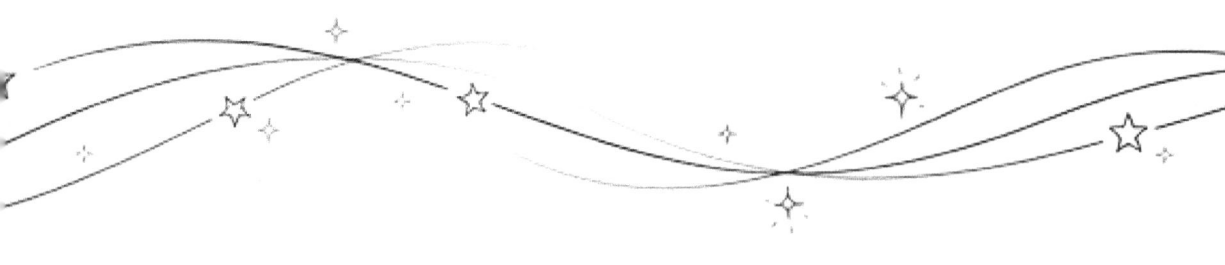

FORTY
Pressure to Be Perfect

Perfection is a trap.

Growth is the goal.

My grace is sufficient for you, for My power is made perfect in weakness.

— **2 CORINTHIANS 12:9**

📖 The "I Can't Mess Up" Feeling

Perfection pressure is exhausting because it never lets you relax. It whispers stuff like:

"If I mess up, everyone will think I'm bad."

"I have to be flawless to be respected."

"I can't make mistakes today."

"I have to prove myself every single time."

And then you play tight, you hesitate, and you overthink. You stop taking smart risks because you are scared to get it wrong.

Here's what 2 Corinthians 12:9 says: God's grace is enough, and His power shows up in weakness. That's a wild idea, especially in sport where everyone is obsessed with looking strong. But God is not shocked by your imperfections. He is not waiting to love you until you are flawless. He knows you are learning, He knows you have limits, and He knows that you are human.

Grace doesn't mean you don't try; it means you stop treating mistakes like a disaster.

Perfectionism says: "One mistake means I'm not good."

Grace says: "One mistake means I'm human, and I can keep going."

While perfectionism makes us feel like we are constantly being graded, grace helps us breathe and stay coachable. This week, you are practicing the mindset shift from perfection to progress.

You don't need to be perfect to be valuable.

You just need to be willing.

Willing to learn. Willing to try. Willing to keep going.

And that is where God's strength will meet you.

🎯 Game-Day Mindset: Progress, Not Perfect

Your goal is not a flawless performance. Your goal is a faithful one.

This Week's Cue Phrase:
💭 **"Grace, then grow."**

Say it after mistakes and after imperfect moments.

🏋️ Training Room Application: The Two Mistakes Rule

This week, when you make a mistake:

1. **First mistake:** "Okay, learn."
2. **Second mistake:** "Okay, adjust."
3. **After that:** no more self-roasting.

Instead, learn to go into action mode: breathe, reset, focus on one simple job.

🍃 Mindset Reps Journal Time

😣 Where do I feel perfection pressure most, sport, school, friendships, or social media?

🪨 What do I say to myself when I make a mistake?

🤍 Write a grace-based self-talk sentence you will use this week.

🎯 What is one area I want progress in, not perfection?

🙏 What weakness do I need to bring to God and trust His grace with?

_____
_____
_____
_____
_____
_____
_____
_____
_____

🙏 Prayer

God, thank You that Your grace is enough for me.

Help me release the pressure to be perfect.

Teach me to learn from mistakes without spiraling into shame.

Give me courage to try, patience to grow, and peace when I'm not flawless.

Let Your strength show up in my weakness.

Amen.

🔥 Weekly Challenge: Grace & Growth

This week, every time you make a mistake:

1. Take one slow breath.
2. Say: **"Grace, then grow."**
3. Choose one adjustment and move on.

After practice or a game, write one sentence:

"Today, I chose progress over perfection when…"

Perfection is loud, but **grace is stronger**. And you are learning to live in that strength.

FORTY-ONE

Staying Humble When You're Winning

Winning is fun, but it's not your identity.
Humility keeps you grounded.

Pride goes before destruction, a haughty spirit before a fall.

— **PROVERBS 16:18**

📖 The Glow-Up Season

Winning feels amazing, doesn't it? You're playing well and your confidence is up. People notice, and your coach praises you. Your team is clicking. It feels like everything is finally working.

But Proverbs 16:18 gives a warning that is basically God saying: "Don't let winning mess with your head." Honestly, success can do weird things to people if they're not careful.

It can make you:

- start acting superior
- forget the people who helped you
- stop working hard because you feel "set"
- treat others like they're below you
- get lazy with your attitude because you think you've "made it"

Pride doesn't always look like bragging. Sometimes it looks like quiet arrogance:

"I'm obviously the best."
"They need me."
"I don't need to listen."
"I don't have to work as hard now."

However, humility is what keeps you steady when things go well.

I'm grateful.
I'll keep working.
I respect others.
I stay coachable.
I don't need to be the centre of everything.

God is not against you succeeding. He's against success owning you. So, this week is about handling wins the right way: with gratitude, respect, and a grounded heart.

🎯 Game-Day Mindset: Gratitude Keeps You Grounded

Winning is a gift, but the way you carry success matters.

This week's cue phrase:

☑ **"Grateful and grounded."**

Say it when you feel tempted to get cocky or compare yourself to others.

🏋 Training Room Application: The Humble Winner Habits

Pick **two** habits to practice this week:

- **Thank someone** who helped you improve (coach, teammate, parent, friend)
- **Celebrate a teammate** out loud, not just yourself
- **Stay coachable** even when you're doing well
- **Keep doing the basics** with full effort (warm-ups, defense, conditioning)
- **No trash talk** even when you're confident
- **Give credit to God** in a simple, real way

Mindset Reps Journal Time

🏆 How do I act when I'm winning or doing well? Be honest.

What is one pride trap I need to watch out for?

Who has helped me grow, and how can I show gratitude?

How can I use my success to lift others instead of lifting myself?

🙏 Ask God to keep your heart humble. What do you want to stay grounded in?

_____
_____
_____
_____
_____
_____
_____
_____
_____
_____
_____
_____

🙏 Prayer

God, thank You for the wins and the growth You've given me.

Help me stay humble and grateful.

Protect me from pride and selfishness.

Teach me to use success to encourage others and honor You.

Keep me grounded, coachable, and kind.

Amen.

🔥 Weekly Challenge: Grateful Winner

This week, after a good game or a win:

1. Thank God for the opportunity and strength.
2. Compliment a teammate for something specific.
3. Ask yourself: "What's one thing I can still improve?"

Then write one sentence:

"This week, I stayed humble by..."

Winning is fun. Humility is wisdom. And you can have both.

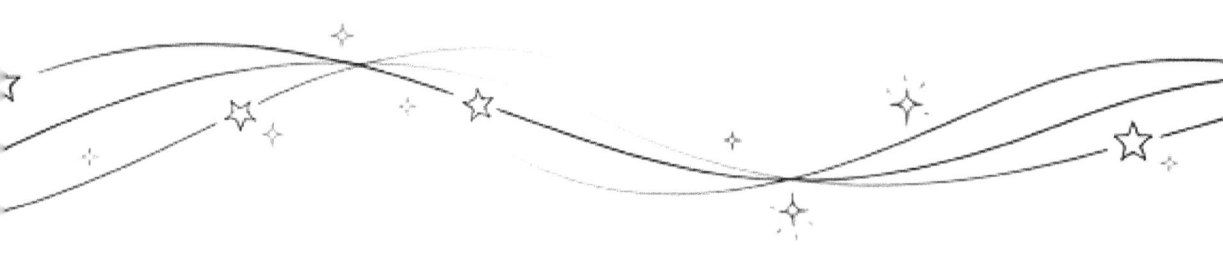

FORTY-TWO
Forgiving Yourself

God's forgiveness is real, and you are allowed
to move forward.

If we confess our sins, He is faithful and just and will forgive us... and purify us.

— 1 JOHN 1:9

📖 When You Can't Stop Cringing at Yourself

Some mistakes fade fast. Others stick in your head like an annoying song you cannot turn off.

Maybe you snapped at a teammate, said something mean, quit on a drill, or acted immature. Maybe you did something you regret and now you keep replaying it.

And the worst part is not always the consequences. Sometimes the worst part is how you talk to yourself afterward.

> "I'm so embarrassing."
> "I ruin everything."
> "I'm a bad person."
> "I don't deserve another chance."

Conviction and shame are not the same thing. Conviction is when God shows you what needs to change, and it leads you to growth. Shame is when you believe you are broken and unworthy, and it tries to keep you stuck.

1 John 1:9 is simple: if we confess, God forgives. Not "maybe." Not "if you earn it." He is faithful, He cleans you up, and He restores you. So, if God forgives you, why do you keep punishing yourself?

Sometimes we hold onto guilt because it feels like paying for it. But guilt is not a payment plan. Jesus already paid.

Forgiving yourself is not ignoring what happened. It is owning it, learning from it, making it right if you can, and then letting it go. Staying stuck will not make you holy; it will just makes you exhausted.

. . .

This week, you are practicing freedom: learning from your mistakes without living in shame.

🎯 Game-Day Mindset: Own It, Then Release It

You can take responsibility without staying trapped in regret.

This Week's Cue Phrase:
☑ **"I'm forgiven, I'm growing."**

🏋️ Training Room Application: The Clean Reset Plan

Use this when you mess up in sport or life.

1. **Own it**: What did I do wrong? Keep it simple. No self-hate speech.

2. **Make it right** (if needed)

    - apologize
    - fix what you can
    - ask for help
    - take responsibility

3. **Confess to God**: "God, I'm sorry for _____. Please forgive me and help me change."

4. **Release it**: Say: "I'm forgiven, I'm growing."
Then do the next right thing.

Mindset Reps Journal Time

- What is something I'm still holding against myself?

- What would it look like to take responsibility without shame?

- Is there anyone I need to apologize to, including myself? What would I say?

- Write a forgiveness statement you want to believe: "Because God forgives me, I can…"

- Ask God for help changing one specific habit or attitude.

_____
_____
_____
_____
_____
_____
_____
_____
_____
_____

🙏 Prayer

God, I'm sorry for the ways I've messed up.

Thank You that You forgive me when I confess.

Help me accept Your forgiveness and stop punishing myself.

Teach me to learn, grow, and make better choices.

Replace shame with peace and courage.

Amen.

🔥 Weekly Challenge: Release the Shame

This week, pick one mistake you keep replaying.

1. Write what happened in one sentence.
2. Write what you learned in one sentence.
3. Confess it to God and ask for help.
4. Write: **"I'm forgiven, I'm growing."**
5. When your brain tries to replay it, repeat the phrase and move on.

At the end of the week, write one sentence:

"This week, I forgave myself by…"

You are not meant to live in shame. You are meant to live free, forgiven, and growing.

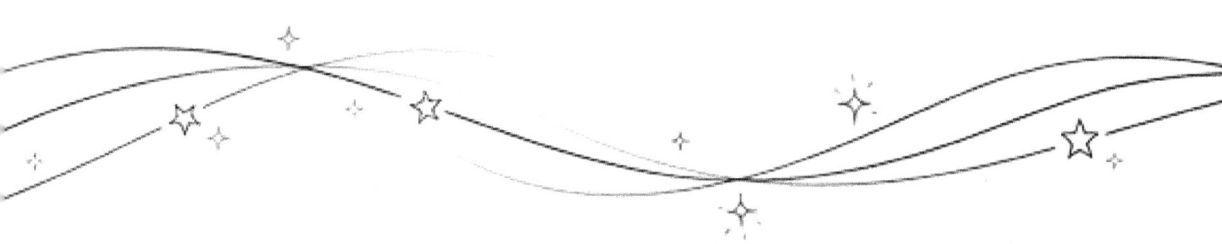

FORTY-THREE
Handling Conflict Like a Leader

Conflict is normal.

How you handle it shows your character.

A gentle answer turns away wrath, but a harsh word stirs up anger.

— **PROVERBS 15:1**

📖 The Awkward Teammate Stuff

Team life is not just drills and games. It's people.

And people can be... a lot. Sometimes conflict looks obvious, like an argument. Sometimes it's quieter, like tension, passive-aggressive comments, side-eyes, group chat drama, or feeling left out.

Frankly, it's easy to handle conflict in ways that make it worse:

- ignoring it until it explodes
- venting to everyone except the person involved
- posting something shady online
- matching someone's attitude
- saying something harsh and regretting it later

Proverbs 15:1 is a simple truth: gentle words can calm things down, harsh words fuel the fire.

Gentle doesn't mean weak.
Gentle means controlled.

A leader doesn't create drama. A leader protects the team. Handling conflict well means you can say hard things in a respectful way. It means you can stand up for yourself without being rude. It means you don't need to "win" the argument, you want to solve the problem.

God cares about your relationships, not just your results. So, this week is about learning how to handle conflict like a leader, not like a reaction.

🎯 Game-Day Mindset: Calm Words, Clear Boundaries

When emotions run hot, your goal is to stay calm and clear.

This week's cue phrase:

☑ **"Gentle and firm."**

🏋️ Training Room Application: The 3-Step Conflict Script

Use this simple approach when you need to address something.

1. **Check your heart first**: Ask: "Am I trying to solve this, or am I trying to hurt them back?"

2. **Use a calm script**

   - "Hey, can we talk for a minute?"
   - "When ___ happened, I felt ___. Can we handle it differently?"
   - "I want us to be good. I just need to clear this up."
   - "I'm not trying to start drama, I just want to fix it."

3. **Ask for a next step**

   - "Can we agree to ___?"
   - "What do you need from me?"
   - "Here's what I'll do. Can you do ___?"

This keeps it focused on solutions rather than blame.

Also, if someone is unsafe or mean, you're allowed to involve a coach or trusted adult.

Peace doesn't mean tolerating disrespect.

Mindset Reps Journal Time

☺ What kind of conflict do I avoid most, awkward conversations, confrontation, or being misunderstood?

🔥 When I'm upset, what is my usual reaction, silent, sarcastic, emotional, or explosive?

✏️ Write one "gentle and firm" sentence I can use if conflict comes up this week.

💭 Is there a relationship I need to repair or clarify? What is one small step I can take?

🙏 Ask God to help you respond with wisdom. What do you need help with most?

_____
_____
_____
_____
_____
_____
_____
_____
_____
_____

🙏 Prayer

God, help me handle conflict with wisdom and self-control.

Teach me to use gentle words and a calm spirit.

Help me set healthy boundaries and seek peace without pretending problems don't exist.

Give me courage to have hard conversations in a respectful way.

Make me a peacemaker and a strong teammate.

Amen.

🔥 Weekly Challenge: Gentle and Firm

This week, if conflict shows up:

1. Take one slow breath.
2. Say: **"Gentle and firm."**
3. Use one calm sentence to address the issue directly.
4. Aim for a solution, not a victory.

Afterward, write one sentence:

"This week, I handled conflict like a leader when…"

Remember: Drama is loud, but leadership is steady.

FORTY-FOUR
Setting Boundaries

Boundaries protect your peace, your focus, and your future.

Above all else, guard your heart, for everything you do flows from it.

— **PROVERBS 4:23**

📖 You're Allowed to Protect Your Peace

Boundaries can sound scary because people sometimes act like boundaries are rude. But boundaries are not rudeness; they are wisdom.

A boundary is simply a decision you make about what you will allow and what you will not allow. It's how you guard your heart, like Proverbs 4:23 says.

Teen life can come with a lot of pressure to say yes:

Yes to drama.
Yes to gossip.
Yes to being available 24/7.
Yes to group chats that never sleep.
Yes to people who take but never give.
Yes to staying up late because you don't want to miss anything.

And then you wonder why you feel drained.

Boundaries protect your energy so you can show up well in the things that matter: your faith, your school, your sport, your health, your relationships. They also protect you from becoming someone you don't want to be.

Sometimes the boundary is with other people:

- "I don't like when you talk to me like that."
- "I'm not comfortable with this."
- "I need space."

Sometimes the boundary is with yourself:

- "I'm not scrolling past 10 pm."
- "I'm not skipping meals."
- "I'm not joining gossip."
- "I'm going to sleep."

. . .

God isn't asking you to be nice in a way that destroys your peace. He's asking you to **be wise** in a way that honors Him.

This week, you're practicing strength through boundaries.

🎯 Game-Day Mindset: Guard What Matters

Boundaries are not walls; they are guardrails.

This Week's Cue Phrase:

☑ **"I guard my heart."**

🏋️ Training Room Application: The Boundary Checklist

Choose **one** boundary to practice this week:

✓ **Phone boundary:** no social media after 9:30 pm

✓ **Sleep boundary:** bedtime routine starts at the same time 3 nights this week

✓ **Gossip boundary:** "I'm not doing that" and change the subject

✓ **Friendship boundary:** stop chasing people who don't treat you well

. . .

✓ **Sport boundary:** protect recovery, stretch after training, fuel properly

✓ **Mental boundary:** stop replaying mistakes after your 10-minute review

✓ **Faith boundary:** 2 minutes with God before bed

Now, write one sentence you'll use if you need to say it out loud:

"I'm not comfortable with that."

"I'm going to sit this one out."

"I need to focus on sleep tonight."

"Let's talk about something else."

Short. Calm. Clear.

Mindset Reps Journal Time

- Where do I feel most drained right now, friends, sport, school, or online life?

- What boundary do I need most, and why?

- Write a simple boundary sentence I can say without being rude.

- What fear makes boundaries hard for me, being disliked, conflict, missing out, or disappointing people?

- Ask God for courage to guard your heart. What do you need His help with?

_____
_____
_____
_____
_____
_____
_____
_____
_____
_____
_____
_____

🙏 Prayer

God, help me guard my heart with wisdom.

Teach me to set boundaries that protect my peace and honor You.

Give me courage to say no when I need to, and strength to stick to my choices.

Help me be kind and clear, not people-pleasing and drained.

Amen.

🔥 Weekly Challenge: One Boundary

This week, practice one boundary every day.

1. Say: **"I guard my heart."**
2. Follow through on your boundary, even if it feels awkward.
3. At the end of the week, write one sentence:

"When I set a boundary, I noticed…"

Boundaries are not selfish. They're stewardship, and you're completely allowed to protect your peace.

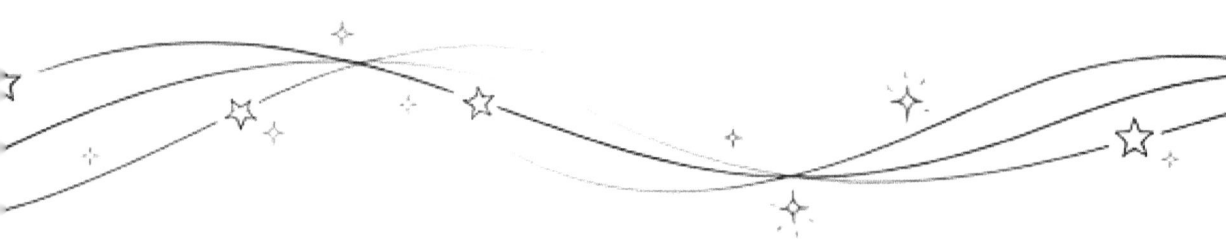

FORTY-FIVE
When You're Not Chosen

Rejection hurts, but it does not get the final word over your future.

The Lord will fulfill His purpose for me.

— **PSALM 138:8**

📖 The Email, the List, the Silence

Getting cut. Not making the team. Being benched. Not being selected for rep. Not getting the starting spot. Even if you pretend you're fine, it stings. Sometimes it feels unfair. Sometimes it feels embarrassing. Sometimes it feels like everyone else is moving forward and you're stuck.

And then your brain starts building a story:

- "I'm not good enough."
- "I'll never get there."
- "Maybe I'm not meant for this."
- "People see something in me and it's not good."

Psalm 138:8 says God will fulfill His purpose for you. That means your purpose is bigger than one coach's decision. Bigger than one tryout, bigger than one season, and bigger than one moment of disappointment. This doesn't mean rejection doesn't hurt. It does. But it means rejection is not the end of your story.

Sometimes, not chosen means:

- you need more time and training
- you need a different environment
- you need growth that only happens in the hidden season
- God is protecting you from something you don't see yet
- your path is going to look different than you expected

A door closing can feel like a judgment, but it can also be direction. So, this week is about staying steady when you're not chosen. It's about letting yourself feel the disappointment, then choosing not to let it define you.

You can grieve it, you can learn from it, and you can keep going.

🎯 Game-Day Mindset: This Is Not the End

One decision does not define your potential.

This week's cue phrase:

☑ **"My purpose is bigger."**

🏋️ Training Room Application: The Rejection Recovery Plan

If you've been rejected, overlooked, or not chosen, try this plan:

1. **Let yourself feel it**. Talk to someone safe. Cry if you need to. Journal it. Do not pretend.

2. **Get one piece of feedback**. If possible, ask:
"What's one thing I can improve to be considered next time?"

3. **Choose one focus goal**. Pick one skill or habit you'll work on for the next 4 weeks.

4. **Pray purpose over yourself**. "God, fulfill Your purpose for me. Help me keep going."

Rejection becomes less powerful when you turn it into a plan.

🌿 Mindset Reps Journal Time

😔 What rejection or disappointment am I dealing with right now?

💭 What story am I telling myself about what it means?

📖 Write a truth statement based on Psalm 138:8 that you want to believe.

🎯 What is one skill or habit I can focus on for the next month?

🙏 What do I need to ask God for right now, comfort, courage, direction, or endurance?

_____
_____
_____
_____
_____
_____
_____
_____
_____
_____
_____

🙏 Prayer

God, this hurts.

I feel disappointed and overlooked.

Thank You that my purpose does not depend on people's choices.

Fulfill Your purpose for me and guide my path.

Give me courage to keep training, keep growing, and keep believing.

Heal my heart and help me move forward with hope.

Amen.

🔥 Weekly Challenge: Plan, Not Panic

This week, if you feel rejected or overlooked:

1. Say: **"My purpose is bigger."**
2. Write one lesson you can learn.
3. Choose one action step you can take.
4. Pray for strength and direction.

Then write one sentence:

"This week, I moved forward by…"

Not being chosen is painful, but it's not permanent. God is still writing your story.

FORTY-SIX
Identity Beyond Sport

You are an athlete, but you are not only an athlete.

You are God's masterpiece.

— **EPHESIANS 2:10**

📖 When Sport Feels Like Your Whole Personality

Sport can be amazing… and also a little dangerous if it becomes your whole identity. Because if your identity is only "the athlete," then what happens when you get injured, benched, or have a bad season? What happens when you stop improving as fast, don't make the team, or change sports?

If sport is your whole identity, those moments can truly feel like losing yourself.

Ephesians 2:10 says you are God's masterpiece. Not "God's masterpiece when you win." Not "God's masterpiece when you're starting." Just… masterpiece. That means your value is not attached to your performance. Your sport is something you do, not who you are.

You have gifts beyond sport:

- your kindness
- your sense of humor
- your creativity
- your leadership
- your loyalty
- your intelligence
- your faith
- your ability to encourage others

God made you with purpose that is bigger than one role on a team. And here's the cool part: when your identity is secure, you actually play better. You play freer. You take smarter risks. You recover faster after mistakes. You don't crumble when things go wrong, because your whole worth is not on the line.

This week, we're strengthening your foundation: who you are in God, not just what you do in sport.

🎯 Game-Day Mindset: Athlete Is a Role, Not a Label

You can care deeply about your sport without making it your whole self.

This Week's Cue Phrase:

☑ **"I am more than my performance."**

🏋 Training Room Application: The Identity List

This week, create your identity list. Not "what I do." **Who I am**.

Write 10 "I am" statements that are not about sport stats.

Examples:

- 🤍 I am loved by God
- 🧠 I am a learner
- 💬 I am a good friend
- 🌱 I am growing
- 💪 I am resilient
- 🎨 I am creative
- ✊ I am brave
- 🧭 I am purposeful
- 🙏 I am not alone
- 🎯 I am becoming who God made me to be

Read your list before games or when you're feeling low.

🥎 Mindset Reps Journal Time

🏐 If I couldn't play my sport for a year, what would I be afraid of losing about myself?

🥎 What do I believe makes me valuable? Where did I learn that?

Write 5 "I am" statements that are true even on a bad game day.

What gifts do I have that have nothing to do with sport?

🙏 Ask God to help you build a secure identity. What do you need to hear from Him?

_____
_____
_____
_____
_____
_____
_____
_____
_____
_____
_____

🙏 Prayer

God, thank You that my value doesn't rise and fall with my performance.

Help me build my identity in You.

Remind me that I am Your masterpiece, created with purpose.

When sport feels like everything, ground me in truth.

Help me play with freedom, because my worth is secure in You.

Amen.

🔥 Weekly Challenge: More Than Sport

This week, do one thing that builds your identity outside sport:

- create something
- read for fun
- spend time with a friend without talking about sport
- write a prayer or gratitude list
- learn a new skill
- try music or journaling

Then, write one sentence:

> **"This week, I remembered I'm more than sport when…"**

Sport is part of your story, but it's not the whole book. God is writing something bigger.

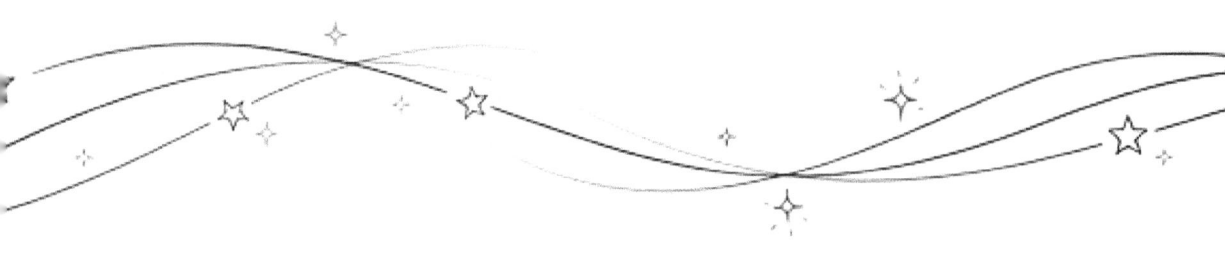

FORTY-SEVEN
When You're Injured or Sidelined

Your value doesn't change when your body needs healing.

He heals the brokenhearted and binds up their wounds.

— **PSALM 147:3**

📖 The Hard Part Isn't Just the Injury

Getting injured is rough, but being sidelined can be even harder. It's often not just dealing with pain, but with so many confronting emotions:

- frustration
- boredom
- FOMO
- feeling useless
- feeling behind
- jealousy watching others play
- fear you won't come back the same

And sometimes people just don't get it. They say things like, "At least you get a break," like being injured is a cute holiday. It's not.

Psalm 147:3 says God heals and binds up wounds. That includes the physical stuff and the heart stuff. Injury can make you feel like you've lost your place, like your identity is shaky, or like you're no longer part of the team. But here's a truth you need this week:

You're still an athlete while you heal.
You're still valuable while you rest.
You're still part of your team while you recover.

Healing is not a pause on your purpose. Healing is part of your journey, and even if you can't train the same way, you can still grow:

- **mentally**, by building patience and resilience
- **spiritually**, by learning trust and surrender
- **relationally**, by becoming a supportive teammate
- **physically**, by committing to rehab with discipline

. . .

This week isn't about rushing back, but about **healing well**. Strong athletes don't just push; they also recover with wisdom.

🎯 Game-Day Mindset: Healing Is Training

Rest is not quitting. Rehab is not "less than." Healing is a form of discipline.

This week's cue phrase:

☑ **"I heal with patience."**

🏋️ Training Room Application: The Sidelined Strategy

If you're injured or limited right now, try this:

Do rehab like it matters, because it does. Stick to your plan. Small consistency beats random intensity.

Stay mentally in the game. Watch practice. Learn plays. Ask questions. Take notes.

Stay connected to your team. Encourage teammates. Celebrate their wins. Be present.

Pray over your healing. "God, help my body heal and help my mind stay steady."

If you're not injured right now, this still matters, as it builds compassion for teammates who are sidelined.

🏐 Mindset Reps Journal Time

😔 If I'm sidelined, what is the hardest part for me, pain, boredom, fear, or feeling left out?

💭 What negative thought keeps showing up, and what truth can replace it?

 What is one rehab or recovery habit I can commit to this week?

 How can I stay a good teammate even when I can't play fully?

🙏 What do I need to ask God for, patience, strength, peace, or hope?

_____
_____
_____
_____
_____
_____
_____
_____
_____
_____

🙏 Prayer

God, thank You that You see me even when I'm sidelined.

Please heal my body and calm my mind.

Help me be patient with the process and disciplined in recovery.

Remind me that my value does not depend on what I can do today.

Give me hope and strength as I heal.

Amen.

🔥 Weekly Challenge: Heal Well

This week, choose one healing action and do it consistently:

- rehab exercises
- sleep and recovery
- hydration
- fueling well
- daily prayer for healing
- encouraging one teammate

At the end of the week, write one sentence:

"This week, I healed well by..."

Your body may need time, but your growth doesn't stop. God is still building you, even in the recovery season.

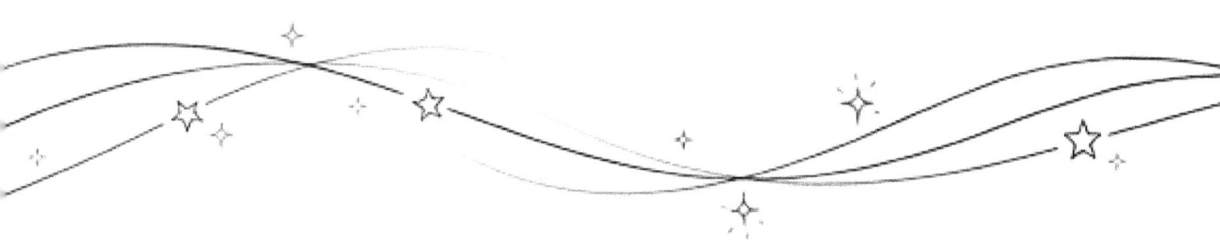

FORTY-EIGHT
Courage to Be Different

You don't have to follow the crowd to belong.

You can follow God and still be confident.

Do not conform to the pattern of this world, but be transformed by the renewing of your mind.

— **ROMANS 12:2**

📖 When Fitting In Feels Like the Whole Game

Being a teen girl can feel like there are unspoken rules you're supposed to follow. Laugh at the right jokes. Wear the right things. Act unbothered. Go along with it so you don't look "weird." Stay quiet so you don't make it awkward.

And team culture can add extra pressure:

If everyone's gossiping, you feel like you have to join in.

If teammates are making bad choices, you feel like you have to pretend it's fine.

If people are teasing someone, you feel like staying silent is safer.

But Romans 12:2 says you don't have to copy the world's pattern. You can choose a different way. The truth is, it takes courage to be different. It takes courage to be kind when others are cruel.

It takes courage to say no when others pressure you. It takes courage to protect your values when everyone wants you to go along with the vibe.

Being different doesn't mean being better than people. It means being faithful. God isn't asking you to be popular, but he *is* asking you to be brave. And bravery is not always loud. Sometimes bravery is simply quietly choosing what's right.

This week is about building the courage to stand out in a healthy way. Not to get attention, but to stay true to who you are in God.

🎯 GAME-DAY MINDSET: I DON'T HAVE TO BLEND IN

You don't need everyone to agree with you to know you're doing the right thing.

THIS WEEK'S CUE PHRASE:

☑ **"I stand with God."**

🏋 TRAINING ROOM APPLICATION: THE DIFFERENT CHOICE PLAN

This week, practice one different choice on purpose.

- Don't join gossip, change the subject
- Say no to pressure that makes you uncomfortable
- Be kind to someone who gets left out
- Set a boundary with social media
- Refuse negative self-talk and replace it with truth
- Take time with God even if no one else does

And if you need a simple line to use, try:

- "Nah, I'm not into that."
- "Let's not talk about her."
- "I'm going to head home."
- "That's not for me."

Mindset Reps Journal Time

☺ Where do I feel the most pressure to fit in, team culture, friends, social media, or school?

🧠 What is one area where I'm tempted to conform, even when it doesn't match my values?

💬 Write one sentence I can use to hold my boundary without being rude.

♡ What is one "different choice" I want to practice this week?

🙏 Ask God to renew your mind. What thought pattern do you want Him to change in you?

_____
_____
_____
_____
_____
_____
_____
_____
_____
_____
_____

🙏 Prayer

God, give me courage to be different in the right ways.

Help me not conform to pressure that pulls me away from You.

Renew my mind and strengthen my values.

Teach me to be kind, brave, and steady.

Help me stand with You even when it feels awkward.

Amen.

🔥 Weekly Challenge: A Different Choice

This week, make one different choice when you feel pressure.

1. Say: **"I stand with God."**
2. Choose the healthy boundary.
3. Do one kind action that reflects your values.

Afterward, write one sentence:

"This week, I was brave when..."

Being different can feel uncomfortable, but it's also how you become strong. God will never leave you standing alone.

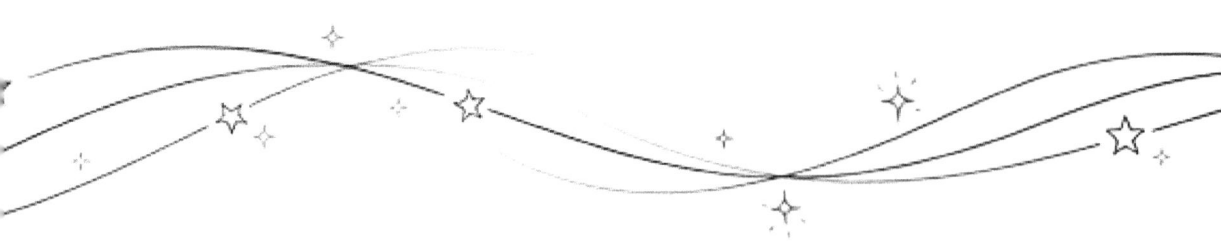

FORTY-NINE

Finishing Strong

Anyone can start.

Finishing takes endurance, faith, and heart.

Let us run with perseverance the race marked out for us.

— **HEBREWS 12:1**

📖 The Middle Is Hard; the Finish Is a Choice

Welcome to week 49! This means that you're in the final stretch, and it's where a lot of people mentally check out. Not because they don't care, but because they're tired. Tired from school. Tired from training. Tired from pressure. Tired from trying to be strong all the time.

The end of a season can feel like:

"I just want this to be over."

"I'm running out of energy."

"I don't think I can keep up."

"I've already messed up, so what's the point?"

Hebrews 12:1 says run with perseverance. That word means you keep going even when it's not fun anymore. Perseverance is not loud, it's stubborn faith. It's showing up when you're tired, doing the basics when you're bored, staying kind when you're stressed, and finishing what you started.

Here's a key truth: finishing strong does not mean finishing perfect. It means you keep your character, you keep your effort, and you keep your faith steady. It means that you don't quit on yourself.

God has a race marked out for you. That means your path is your path, and you don't need to run someone else's race. You don't need to copy someone else's pace. You just need to keep moving forward on the track God set for you.

This week is about ending with endurance.

🎯 Game-Day Mindset: Endurance Is a Decision

You don't need to feel strong to choose strong.

This Week's Cue Phrase:

✅ "I finish strong."

🏋️ Training Room Application: The Final Stretch Plan

Choose one "finish strong" habit for this week:

- **Last 10 minutes effort:** no coasting at the end of practice
- **Reset fast:** do not spiral after mistakes
- **Leadership:** encourage teammates when everyone is tired
- **Recovery:** sleep and hydrate so you don't fade late
- **Faith:** pray before practice, even if it's short
- **Consistency:** do your minimum standard daily

When you feel tired, don't negotiate with your goals. Just simplify and execute.

Mindset Reps Journal Time

- Where do I usually fade, mentally, physically, emotionally, or spiritually?

- What excuse shows up when I'm tired, and what is my better response?

- What is my "finish strong" habit for this week? Make it specific.

- What does finishing strong look like for me, effort, attitude, leadership, or faith?

- Ask God for perseverance. What do you need strength for right now?

_____
_____
_____
_____
_____
_____
_____
_____
_____
_____
_____

🙏 Prayer

God, give me perseverance.

When I'm tired, help me keep going with faith and courage.

Help me run my race with endurance and not quit on myself.

Strengthen my body, steady my mind, and guard my heart.

Teach me to finish strong with integrity and joy.

Amen.

🔥 Weekly Challenge: No Coasting

This week, choose one practice or game where you will focus on finishing strong.

1. Say: **"I finish strong."**
2. Give your best effort in the final 10 minutes.
3. Encourage one teammate when they look tired.
4. Afterward, write one sentence:

"Today, I finished strong when…"

Your future isn't built by the days you feel amazing; it's built by the days you keep going anyway.

FIFTY
Trusting God with the Outcome

Do your part with excellence, then
release the results to God.

Commit to the Lord whatever you do, and He will establish your plans.

— **PROVERBS 16:3**

📖 THE RESULTS OBSESSION

At this point in the year, outcomes can feel extra loud. There are finals, championships, selections, rankings, tryouts, awards, stats, and many decisions. And even if you try to be chill, your brain probably still whispers:

"What if it doesn't work out?"

"What if I don't get picked?"

"What if we lose?"

"What if I trained for nothing?"

Here's the hard truth: you can do everything right and still not get the outcome you wanted. That's not failure; it's just life. Proverbs 16:3 tells you to commit your work to the Lord. Notice what it does not say. It does not promise you'll win every game or get every spot. It promises God will establish your plans. He will guide you, strengthen you, grow you, and direct your path.

Trusting God with the outcome means you stop trying to control what you cannot control. It means you can play hard without panicking, prepare without being obsessed, and want something without worshipping it. And yes, it's normal to care. Wanting to win is fine. Wanting to achieve is fine.

But outcomes make a terrible god. When you worship outcomes, you live anxious. When you commit your work to God, you live steadier. Because God cares about who you become, not just what you achieve. This week is about release. Do your part. Pray.

Then **let go** of the rest.

🎯 Game-Day Mindset: Do Your Part, Release the Rest

This Week's Cue Phrase:

✅ **"Committed and released."**

Committed = I prepared and gave effort.

Released = I trust God with what happens next.

🏋️ Training Room Application: The Outcome Release Routine

Use this before games, tryouts, or tests.

1. Write your controllables (3 things)
Examples: effort, focus, communication.

2. Commit them to God
"God, I commit my effort, focus, and attitude to You."

3. Release one outcome
Name it: "I release the need to ____."
Examples:

- "I release the need to be perfect."
- "I release the need to impress everyone."
- "I release the fear of losing."

4. Choose your next right step

Mindset Reps Journal Time

- What outcome am I most anxious about right now?

- What are 3 controllables I can commit to God this week?

- What do I need to release because it's not mine to control?

- How does outcome obsession affect how I play, study, or live?

- Write a short prayer committing your plans to God.

_____
_____
_____
_____
_____
_____
_____
_____
_____
_____
_____
_____

🙏 Prayer

God, I commit my work to You.

Help me do my part with excellence and integrity.

Free me from outcome obsession and fear.

Teach me to trust You with what happens next.

Establish my plans and guide my path.

Give me peace, courage, and joy as I show up.

Amen.

🔥 Weekly Challenge: Release

This week, before every practice or game:

1. Say: **"Committed and released."**
2. Choose one controllable to focus on.
3. Release one outcome to God.

Afterward, write one sentence:

"Today, I trusted God with the outcome when…"

You were never meant to carry results like they decide your worth. Do your part, trust God, and let the rest go.

FIFTY-ONE
Gratitude in Every Season

Gratitude isn't only for winning.

It's for becoming.

Give thanks in all circumstances; for this is God's will for you in Christ Jesus.

— 1 THESSALONIANS 5:18

📖 THE SEASON YOU DIDN'T EXPECT

By Week 51, you've lived a lot of moments. Some were amazing. Some were disappointing. Some were awkward.

Some were proud tears.

Some were frustrated tears.

Some were "I can't believe I did that" moments.

Some were "I can't believe that happened" moments.

It's easy to look back and only thank God for the highlights. The wins, the good days, and the compliments. But 1 Thessalonians 5:18 says give thanks in all circumstances. Not because every circumstance is good, but because God can still be good in every circumstance.

Gratitude is not pretending you enjoyed the hard parts; it's noticing that even in the hard parts, you were not alone. Maybe you learned resilience, humility, and boundaries. Maybe you learned who your real friends are, and how to breathe through pressure.

Maybe you even learned how to bounce back, and that your worth isn't a scoreboard.

God doesn't waste seasons. Even the messy ones. When you practice gratitude, it changes your focus. You stop living like everything is missing, and you start seeing what's been growing. And honestly, gratitude is one of the fastest ways to get your peace back.

This week is about looking back with a grateful heart, not a critical one.

🎯 Game-Day Mindset: Gratitude Grounds You

Gratitude helps you stay humble when you win and hopeful when you don't.

This week's cue phrase:
✅ **"Thankful and steady."**

🏋️ Training Room Application: The 3-Part Gratitude Practice

Do this once a day this week. It takes 2 minutes.

1. **Thank God for one good thing.** Something small counts.
2. **Thank God for one growth thing.** Something you learned, even from a hard moment.
3. **Thank someone.** A teammate, coach, parent, friend, teacher. A quick message counts.

Gratitude multiplies joy and heals bitterness.

Mindset Reps Journal Time

What is one moment this year that I'm genuinely grateful for?

What is one hard moment that helped me grow? What did it teach me?

Who helped me this year, and how can I thank them?

What do I tend to focus on that steals gratitude from me, comparison, negativity, or perfectionism?

Write a short prayer of thanks in all circumstances, even the tough ones.

_____
_____
_____
_____
_____
_____
_____
_____
_____
_____
_____

🙏 Prayer

God, thank You for being with me in every season.

Thank You for the wins, the lessons, and the growth.

Help me be grateful in all circumstances, not because everything is easy, but because You are faithful.

Teach me to notice the good, learn from the hard, and stay steady in You.

Amen.

🔥 Weekly Challenge: Three Thanks

Every day this week write three quick thanks:

1. One thing you're grateful for today
2. One way you're growing
3. One person you appreciate

At the end of the week, write one sentence:

> **"This week, gratitude changed my mindset by…"**

Gratitude doesn't erase hard things. It helps you see God's faithfulness through them, and that's a strength that lasts.

FIFTY-TWO
Your Next Season

This is only the beginning.

What God started, He can grow.

He who began a good work in you will carry it on to completion.

— **PHILIPPIANS 1:6**

📖 The Ending That's Actually a Beginning

Week 52 is a finish line, but it's also a beginning. A year of devotions has made you stronger than you were, wiser, more grounded, and more aware of God's presence in your sport and in your life.

Philippians 1:6 is such a steady promise: God finishes what He starts. That means your growth isn't fragile. It means your progress isn't random. It means your future isn't built on one good week or one bad week.

God has been working in you through every part of this year: the wins, the losses, the hard practices, the awkward team moments, the setbacks, the confidence rebuilds, the boundaries, the courage, the faith.

And now you get to step into your next season with more tools, more resilience, and more truth. Here's something important: your next season will probably include new challenges.

New pressure.

New teammates.

New goals.

New opportunities.

There will also be new fears, and moments where you'll need to choose faith again. But that doesn't have to scare you, because you don't actually have to be fully ready; you just have to be willing. You are not becoming an athlete who never struggles. You're becoming an athlete who knows how to respond. You're learning how to reset, how to breathe, how to pray, and how to stand up again.

. . .

This week, instead of obsessing over what could go wrong, you're going to look forward with faith. God started something in you, and He will keep building it.

🎯 GAME-DAY MINDSET: I'M STILL BECOMING

You don't have to have everything figured out. You just need to keep walking forward with God.

THIS WEEK'S CUE PHRASE:
✅ **"God is building me."**

🏋️ TRAINING ROOM APPLICATION: YOUR NEXT SEASON PLAN

Take 10 minutes this week and write your <u>Next Season Plan</u>. Keep it simple.

1. **One goal for my sport**. Make it specific.

2. **One goal for my mindset**: quicker resets, stronger self-talk, calm under pressure.

3. **One goal for my faith**: daily prayer, weekly Bible time, trusting God with outcomes.

4. **One goal for my character**: kindness, coachability, integrity, leadership.

Then choose one habit you'll start this week that supports your goals. Small steps create big change.

🪶 Mindset Reps Journal Time

▦ What is one thing I'm proud of from this year, in sport, faith, or character?

🕊 What is one area where I want to grow next season?

◎ Write one clear goal for sport and one for mindset.

🙏 How has God been shaping me through challenges?

♡ Write a sentence you want to carry into your next season.

_____
_____
_____
_____
_____
_____
_____
_____
_____
_____
_____
_____

🙏 Prayer

God, thank You for carrying me through this year.

Thank You for the growth You've started in me.

As I step into a new season, give me courage, wisdom, and steady faith.

Help me keep becoming who You made me to be.

Lead my steps, strengthen my heart, and keep working in me.

Amen.

🔥 Weekly Challenge: The Next Step

This week, take one small step toward your next season.

1. Say: **"God is building me."**
2. Do one action that matches your goals.
3. Write one sentence:

   "My next season starts now because I…"

You've made it to the end of this journey, which is only the beginning. You made it not just as an athlete, but as a **growing**, **courageous**, **faith-filled** young woman.

I'm so proud of you.

And God? He's always here for you, and he's only getting started.

Keep Going, Girl

As you step into what's next, I want to pause and notice this: **you stayed**. You kept showing up through busy weeks, tired days, and moments when your faith or confidence felt a little shaky. You didn't need perfect focus or perfect weeks to keep turning the pages. After all, consistency isn't about having it all together; it's about choosing to come back again and again.

Over these 52 weeks, I hope you've started to see something the world forgets to tell girls far too often: your worth is not a scoreboard. It isn't a coach's opinion, a highlight reel, a starting spot, a selection list, a number on a scale, or the way you look in a uniform. Your sport is a place where you can grow, learn, and compete with heart, but it was never meant to become the thing that decides whether you are valuable.

There will be seasons when you feel unstoppable, and there will be seasons when you feel unsure. You will experience wins that feel like lightness in your chest and losses that sting longer than you expected, and you'll have days when confidence is strong and days when it feels like it vanished overnight. None of that disqualifies you. It simply means you are human, and you are still becoming.

I hope you always remember that you can **reset after mistakes**, that you can **breathe your way back to calm**, that you can **train your self-talk**, and that you can **lead with strength and kindness** at the same time. I hope you have learned how to hold your standards high without living anxious, how to work hard without burning out, and how to trust God with outcomes you cannot control.

As you step into your next season, don't chase success as if it's the only thing that matters. Chase faithfulness, chase character, and chase the kind of strength that lasts longer than a trophy. Play with purpose, train with wisdom, and let your life reflect the God who is shaping you into someone steady, courageous, and whole.

Whatever happens next, you can move forward with confidence, because God started a good work in you, and He is not finished yet.

www.ingramcontent.com/pod-product-compliance
Lightning Source LLC
Chambersburg PA
CBHW051350070526
44584CB00025B/3707